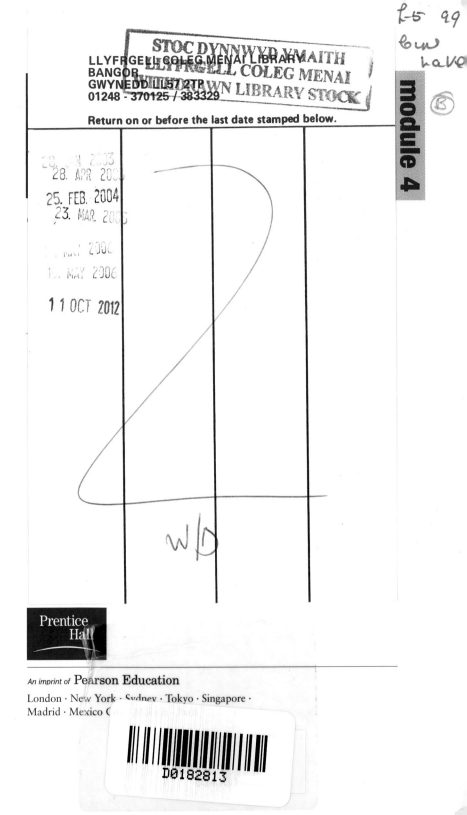

£-5 99
bw
have

module 4

Prentice
Hall

An imprint of Pearson Education

London · New York · Sydney · Tokyo · Singapore ·
Madrid · Mexico C

D0182813

PEARSON EDUCATION LIMITED

Head Office:
Edinburgh Gate
Harlow CM20 2JE
Tel: +44 (0)1279 623623
Fax: +44 (0)1279 431059

London Office:
128 Long Acre
London WC2E 9AN
Tel: +44 (0)20 7447 2000
Fax: +44 (0)20 7240 5771

Website: www.it-minds.com

This edition published in Great Britain in 2002
First published in Great Britain in 2002 as part of *ECDL3 The Complete Coursebook for Microsoft Office 2000*

© Rédacteurs Limited 2002

ISBN 0-130-35461-9

British Library Cataloguing in Publication Data
A CIP catalogue record for this book can be obtained from the British Library

'European Computer Driving Licence' and ECDL and Stars device are registered trademarks of the European Computer Driving Licence Foundation Limited. Rédacteurs Limited is an independent entity from the European Computer Driving Licence Foundation Limited, and not affiliated with the European Computer Driving Licence Foundation in any manner.

This book may be used in assisting students to prepare for the European Computer Driving Licence examination. Neither the European Computer Driving Licence Foundation Limited, Rédacteurs Limited nor the publisher warrants that the use of this book will ensure passing the relevant examination.

Use of the ECDL-F approved Courseware logo on this product signifies that it has been independently reviewed and approved in complying with the following standards:

Acceptable coverage of all courseware content related to ECDL syllabus Module 4 version 3.0. This courseware material has not been reviewed for technical accuracy and does not guarantee that the end user will pass the associated ECDL examinations. Any and all assessment tests and/or performance based exercises contained in these Modular books relate solely to these books and do not constitute, or imply, certification by the European Driving Licence Foundation in respect of any ECDL examinations. For details on sitting ECDL examinations in your country please contact the local ECDL licensee or visit the European Computer Driving Licence Foundation Limited web site at http://www.ecdl.com.

References to the European Computer Driving Licence (ECDL) include the International Computer Driving Licence (ICDL).

ECDL Foundation Syllabus Version 3.0 is published as the official syllabus for use within the European Computer Driving Licence (ECDL) and International Computer Driving Licence (ICDL) certification programmes.

Rédacteurs Limited is at http://www.redact.ie

Brendan Munnelly is at http://www.munnelly.com

10 9 8 7 6 5 4 3 2 1

Typeset by Pantek Arts Ltd, Maidstone, Kent.
Printed and bound in Great Britain by Ashford Colour Press, Gosport, Hampshire.

The Publishers' policy is to use paper manufactured from sustainable forests.

Preface

The European Computer Driving Licence (ECDL) is an internationally recognized qualification in end-user computer skills. It is designed to give employers and job-seekers a standard against which they can measure competence – not in theory, but in practice. Its seven Modules cover the areas most frequently required in today's business environment. More than one million people in over fifty countries have undertaken ECDL in order to benefit from the personal, social and business advantages and international mobility that it provides.

In addition to its application in business, the ECDL has a social and cultural purpose. With the proliferation of computers into every aspect of modern life, there is a danger that society will break down into two groups – the information 'haves' and the information 'have nots'. The seven modules of the ECDL are not difficult, but they equip anyone who passes them to participate actively and fully in the Information Society.

The ECDL is not product-specific – you can use any hardware or software to perform the tasks in the examinations. And you can take the seven examinations in any order, and work through the syllabus at your own pace.

This book is one of a set of seven, each dealing with one of the ECDL modules. While each book can be used independently, if you are new to computers, you should read Module 2: *Using a computer and managing files* before attempting any of the other practical modules (such as this one). Module 2 teaches you the basic operations that are needed in the other practical modules.

The examples in these books are based on PCs (rather than Apple Macintoshes), and on Microsoft software, as follows:
- Operating system: Microsoft Windows 95/98
- Word Processing: Microsoft Word 2000
- Spreadsheets: Microsoft Excel 2000
- Databases: Microsoft Access 2000
- Presentations: Microsoft PowerPoint 2000
- Information and Communication: Microsoft Internet Explorer 5.0 and Microsoft Outlook Express 5.0

If you use other hardware or software, you can use the principles discussed in this book, but the details of operation will differ.

Welcome to the world of computers!

CONTENTS

0 5 4 7 3 1

Introduction

S ome things are easy to explain or describe – but difficult to use or operate. A spreadsheet is not one of those things. In fact, it's the very opposite.

At the end of this module, you will be able to build number-crunching spreadsheets for recording, analysing and drawing graphs of just about any kind of numbers you can think of.

A quarterly sales commission, the annual rainfall, or the monthly household budget: if you can count it now, you will be able to put it on a spreadsheet later.

Along the way we will show you the shortcuts that will help you to get a lot of work done on long numbers, but with little typing, and in a very short time.

But you will be no closer to being able to give a one-sentence definition of what exactly a spreadsheet is.

Perhaps it's because spreadsheets are about processing numbers rather than words that they are so hard to define.

Think of this module as your chance to count rather than be counted. Good luck with it.

CHAPTER 1

Your first steps in Excel

In this chapter

'Why do I need to know all this ... What is the point?' You may find yourself asking such questions when reading this chapter.

But first lessons are like that – whether you are learning the guitar, karate or spreadsheets.

In your first hour you usually have the hard work of remembering new activities and words – but rarely the pleasure of putting your new knowledge into practice.

There is nothing in this chapter that you will find difficult or complex. We have included only the material that you really need to know, and we have introduced it as gently as possible.

Halfway through Chapter 2, when you discover the power and convenience of spreadsheets, you will be asking a very different question: 'How did I ever manage to organize my work or life without Microsoft Excel!'

New skills

At the end of this chapter you should be able to:
- Start and quit Excel
- Explain the difference between a worksheet and a workbook
- Create and name Excel worksheets
- Enter numbers, text and cell references to a worksheet
- Edit and delete the contents of a cell
- Use Excel's Undo feature to reverse commands and cell entries
- Save, name, open, create and close Excel workbooks
- Use Excel's online help

New words

At the end of this chapter you should be able to explain the following terms:
- Worksheet
- Workbook
- Cell reference
- Active cell
- Row
- Column
- Cell
- Name box
- Dependent cell

Starting Excel

- Double click on the Microsoft Excel icon.

Microsoft
Excel

  –or–

- Choose **Start | Programs | Microsoft Excel.**

Excel starts and displays a new workbook with three
worksheets ready for you to use.

Worksheets and workbooks

This ECDL Module is about spreadsheets. But Excel does not
use the word spreadsheet. Instead, it uses two other words –
worksheet and workbook. Let's explain what these mean.

Worksheet

*A page that is made up of little boxes arranged in rows
and columns. Relationships can be created between the
cells so that changing the contents of one cell affects the
contents of the related cells.*

In Excel, a worksheet is a spreadsheet. A worksheet is much
larger than your screen. You can see only a very small part of
it at one time.

Workbook

A file containing worksheets.

When you create a new workbook, Excel creates three blank worksheets inside that workbook. Excel calls the worksheets Sheet1, Sheet2 and Sheet3.

An Excel worksheet

To move from one worksheet to another, click the tab that displays its name

If three worksheets are not enough, you can add more to your workbook – up to a maximum of 256. Think of worksheets as pages in a book, and the workbook as the book containing those pages.

Now you will learn the names of the important parts of a worksheet.

Cells

The little boxes that make up a worksheet.

Cells are arranged in (horizontal) rows and (vertical) columns.

Active cell

The cell in which the cursor is currently located.

Only one cell on a worksheet can be the active cell at any one time. You will always know which cell is the active cell: Excel surrounds it with a thicker border. You can make a cell active by clicking on it with the mouse.

The active cell  *A cell that is not the active cell*

When you open a new workbook, Excel makes the top-left cell of the first worksheet, Sheet1, the active cell.

Each worksheet contains 256 columns. Excel names each column with a letter or group of letters.

Column

A vertical line of cells from the top of the worksheet to the bottom.

A worksheet column

The first 26 are named A to Z.

The remainder are AA to AZ, BA to BZ, and continuing through to IA through to IV.

Row

A horizontal line of cells that stretches left-to-right across a worksheet.

A worksheet row

Each worksheet contains 65,536 rows. Excel gives each row a number, from 1 to 65536. The total number of cells in a worksheet is therefore 256 multiplied by 65,536 or 16,777,216!

Each cell in a worksheet has a unique address or location known as its cell reference.

Cell reference

The location or 'address' of a cell on a worksheet.

A cell reference is made up of two parts:

- The column letter (A, B, C, ...)

- The row number (1, 2, 3, ...)

When you open a new workbook in Excel, the active cell is the one on Sheet1 with the cell reference A1.

Remember: column letter first, row number second. For example, B6, C8 and J12.

Column letters: upper- or lower-case?

You will always see cell references written with the column letters in upper-case letters (for example, A1, B10 and W90) rather than in lower-case ones (for example, a1, b10 and w90). This is true for Excel's online help – and this book.

However, when you type a cell reference into Excel, as you will in Exercise 1.1, it does not matter whether you type the column letter in upper- or lower-case. Excel accepts either. You may find it easier to enter column letters in lower-case, because you need to type only the letter key, and not the letter key in combination with the Shift key.

Name box

> *The rectangular area above the top-left corner of a worksheet in which Excel displays the cell reference of the active cell.*

You can use the name box to move the cursor to any cell on the worksheet, making that cell the active cell.

To do so, type the cell reference in the name box and press Enter.

Exercise 1.1: Name box and cell references

Perform this exercise to learn how to enter a cell reference in the name box.

1 Click in the name box.

2 Type B2 and press Enter.

   Excel responds by making cell B2 the active cell.

   As further practice, repeat these two steps for the following cells: D8, A3, H5 and I19.

Entering numbers in cells

When you type something into a cell and press Enter, Excel looks at your entry and asks:

- Is this a number?

- Is this text?

- Is this a cell reference?

- Is this a calculation?

Excel treats each type of entry in a different way. In this chapter you will deal with entering numbers, text and cell references.

Excel accepts two kinds of calculations: formulas (you will learn about these in Chapter 2) and functions (covered in Chapter 3).

Exercise 1.2: Entering a number in a cell

1 Click on B3, making it the active cell.

2 Type the number 1274.

3 Press Enter.

Why does Excel right-align numbers?

In Exercise 1.2, Excel did two things after you pressed Enter.

- It moved 1274 from the left of cell B3 to the right. This is because Excel assumes that you will want to perform addition and other arithmetic operations on the entered number. When you write a list of numbers on paper to add them, you line up the numbers from the right. Excel right-aligns numbers for the same reason.

- It moved the cursor down to cell B4, the cell under B3. Again, this is because of arithmetic. Excel assumes that you will want to enter another number beneath the previous one.

Entering text in a cell

You can enter text in a worksheet as well as numbers. By using text to identify the meaning or source of numbers, you make your worksheet easier to read and understand.

Exercise 1.3: Entering Text in a Cell

1   Click on B2, making it the active cell.

2   Type the word: Add.

3   Press Enter.

	A	B
1		
2		Add
3		1274
4		
5		

Notice how Excel responded after you pressed Enter.

- 'Add' remained in the left of the cell B2. While Excel right-aligns numbers, it left-aligns text.

- It moved the cursor down to cell B3, the cell under B2. Excel assumes that this is the next cell you will want to use.

Text that describes a number on a worksheet is known as a label.

Label

> *A piece of text in a worksheet cell that provides information about the number in an accompanying cell, usually either below it or to its right.*

Entering a cell reference in a cell

Another type of entry you can make in a cell is a cell reference – that is, the address of another cell – preceded by the 'equals' (=) sign. When you do so, Excel reproduces the content of the other cell in the active cell.

Exercise 1.4: Entering a cell reference in a cell

If B3 does not contain the number 1274 from Exercise 1.2, enter it now.

1   Click on cell B10, type the following, and press Enter:

=B3

The Equals key is to the left of the Backspace key

That is, an 'equals' sign (=) followed by cell reference B3.

Excel responds by displaying the current content of B3 (that is, the number 1274) in B10.

The arrow keys

So far you have used the mouse and the name box to move the cursor around the worksheet.

The four arrow keys

Another way of moving the cursor is by pressing the arrow keys. You may find this method faster than moving and clicking the mouse, because you need not take either hand away from the keyboard.

Editing the content of a cell

Sometimes, you will want to change the content of a cell. Exercise 1.5 shows you how.

Exercise 1.5: Editing the content of a cell

1   Double-click on B3.

Excel makes the cell border thinner and displays a blinking cursor in the cell. (The location of the cursor within the cell depends on which part of the cell you double-clicked on.)

2   Using the arrow keys, move the blinking
    cursor to the left of the 4.

3   Press Delete once, deleting the 4.

4   Type 5.

5   Press Enter.

    This moves the cursor out of B3 and down
    to B4. Excel has replaced 1274 with 1275.
    Notice that the number in B10 also changes.

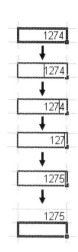

Dependent cells

Cell B10 is an example of a dependent
cell – a cell whose content depends
on the content of another cell. In
this case, the other cell is B3.

When B3 changed from 1274 to
1275, so too did B10. That is because
B10 contains the cell reference of =B3.

As you will learn in later chapters
of this module, cell relationships are
the basis of spreadsheets.

	A	B
1		
2		Add
3		1275
4		
5		
6		
7		
8		
9		
10		1275

*Content of B10 depends
on the content of B3*

F2: Excel's Edit key

In Exercise 1.5 you double-clicked on cell B3. This
made the cell editable – that is, you were able to move
the cursor within the cell and change the cell content.

When a cell is already the active cell, you can make it editable by pressing F2. This is Excel's Edit key. You may find this method faster than double-clicking with the mouse.

Deleting the content a cell

Want to delete a number, text or cell reference from a cell? The following exercise shows you how.

Exercise 1.6: Deleting the Content of a Cell

1   Move the cursor to cell B10. From Exercises 1.4 and 1.5, this contains the cell reference =B3 and displays the number 1275.

2   Press Backspace or Delete.

Excel removes the content of the cell. B10 is now empty.

Deleting and the Enter key

When you enter something to a cell, you must press Enter to confirm the new content of the cell. Similarly, when you edit a cell, Excel makes the change only after you press Enter.

When deleting a cell's content, however, you do not need to press Enter to confirm the deletion. Just pressing Backspace or Delete is enough.

Deleting cell content – not the cell

Another way to delete the content of a
cell is to right-click on the cell and
choose **Clear Contents** from the
pop-up menu.

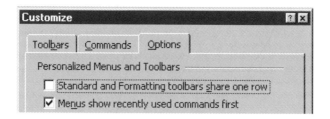

Do not choose **Delete** from this pop-up menu. This
command not only deletes the cell contents – it also removes
the cell itself from the worksheet! As a result, other cells must
change their position to fill the space left empty.

Excel's toolbars

Excel's toolbars give you convenient, one-click access to the
commands that you use most often. By default, Excel displays
just two toolbars, the Standard and Formatting toolbars, on a
single row across the top of the screen.

To display them as two, individual toolbars, follow these steps:

- Choose **Tools | Customize** and click the **Options** tab.

- Deselect the Standard and Formatting toolbars share
  one row checkbox, and choose **Close**.

Hiding and displaying toolbars

You can display or hide Excel's various toolbars by choosing the **View | Toolbars** command, and then selecting or deselecting the various toolbar options from the drop-down menu displayed.

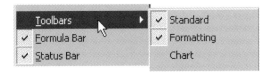

The check marks beside the Standard and Formatting toolbars indicate that they are already selected for display on screen.

The Standard and Formatting toolbars

Only two of Excel's toolbars are relevant to this ECDL module: the Standard toolbar and the Formatting toolbar.

Excel's Standard toolbar

The Standard toolbar includes buttons for managing files and working with numbers in cells.

Excel's Formatting toolbar

The Formatting toolbar includes buttons for changing the appearance of text and numbers in cells.

Rather than introduce all these buttons at once, we will explain the ones you need to know about as they become relevant through the remainder of this ECDL Spreadsheet module.

Hiding and displaying toolbar buttons

You can remove one or more buttons from a toolbar. Follow these steps:

- Display the toolbar that you want to change.

- Hold down the Alt key, and drag the button off the toolbar.

Excel removes the selected button from the toolbar. Want the button back again? Follow this procedure:

- Display the toolbar. Click on **More Buttons** (at the very end of the toolbar) and then on **Add or Remove Buttons**.

- Click the button you want to display again.

- Click anywhere outside the menu to close it.

Excel redisplays the button on the toolbar.

Excel's personalized menus

By default, when you first choose a menu, Excel displays only *some* of the commands on that menu. To view a complete list, click the double-arrow at the bottom of the menu.

If you choose a command that is not displayed by default, Excel adds it to the displayed list the next time you choose the menu.

To view *all* commands each time you choose a menu, follow these steps:

- Choose **Tools | Customize** and click the **Options** tab.

- Deselect the Menus show recently used commands first option, and choose **Close**.

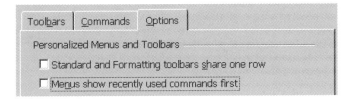

Excel's Undo

Enter the wrong data? Press the wrong key? Don't panic. Excel allows you to undo your most recent cell entry or action if it has produced unwanted results. To undo a cell entry or action:

Undo and Redo buttons

- Choose **Edit | Undo.**

  –or–

- Click the Undo button on the Standard toolbar.

Pressing Undo repeatedly reverses your last series of actions. To view a list of recent actions that you can undo, click the arrow at the right of the Undo button. If you undo an action and then change your mind, click the Redo button (to the right of the Undo button).

Exercise 1.7: Using the Undo feature

Perform this exercise to practise using Excel's Undo feature.

1   Click in cell B2, and press Delete.

2   Click in cell B3, and press Delete.

    Everything that you entered in the worksheet is now deleted! But you can use Undo to get it all back by reversing your two delete actions.

3   Click the Undo button.

    This reverses your most recent action (in Step 2 above). B3 again contains the number 1275.

4   Click Undo a second time.

    This reverses your second most recent action (Step 1 above). B2 again contains the word Add.

Working with Excel workbooks

An Excel workbook is a file containing a collection of
worksheets. The file names of Excel workbooks end in .xls.
This helps you to distinguish Excel files from other file types,
such as Word files (ending in .doc).

Saving your workbook

In Excel, as in other applications, always save your work as
you go along. Don't wait until you are finished! To
save a workbook:

Save button

• Choose **File | Save**.

  –or–

• Click the Save button on the Standard toolbar.

The first time that you save a workbook file, Excel asks you to
give the file a name. Exercise 1.8 shows you how.

Exercise 1.8: Saving and naming a new workbook

1 Sheet1 of your workbook should contain the word 'Add'
   in cell B2 and the number 1275 in cell B3, as entered in
   this chapter's exercises.

   If it does not, enter that data now.

2 Choose **File | Save** or click the Save button on the
   Standard toolbar. Excel displays a dialog box with two
   boxes similar to the ones shown.

File name:	Book1.xls	▼
Save as type:	Microsoft Excel Workbook (*.xls)	▼

Microsoft Excel Workbook (*.xls)
Template (*.xlt)
Formatted Text (Space delimited) (*.prn)
Text (Tab delimited) (*.txt)
Microsoft Excel 5.0/95 Workbook (*.xls)
Microsoft Excel 97 & 5.0/95 Workbook (*.xls)

3   By default, Excel names the first workbook file you open
as Book1.xls. Replace this file name with something that
you will find easier to remember and recognize – such
as your own name – and click the Save button.

File name:	KenBloggs|	▼

Excel adds the file name extension of .xls automatically.
You need not type it.

Creating a new workbook

To create a new workbook file, choose **File | New**.
Alternatively, click the New button on the
Standard toolbar.

New button

Opening an existing workbook

You can have multiple Excel workbooks open at the same
time. To open an existing workbook file:

• Choose **File | Open**.

  –or–

Open button

• Click the Open button on the Standard toolbar. Select
the file you want from the dialog box.

Closing a workbook

To close a workbook file:

- Choose **File | Close**.

  –or–

- Click the Close button at the top right of the workbook window.

If you have made changes to your workbook since you last saved it, Excel prompts you to save the changes before it closes the file.

Exercise 1.9: Closing and reopening a saved workbook

In this exercise you will close and then reopen the workbook you saved in Exercise 1.8.

1 Choose **File | Close** or click the Workbook Close button at the top-right of the workbook window.

2 Choose **File | Open** or click the Open button on the Standard toolbar to display the File Open dialog box. Locate your workbook and open it.

Quitting Excel

To leave Excel:

- Choose **File | Exit**.

  –or–

- Click the Close button at the top right of the Excel window.

If you have left open any files containing unsaved work, Excel prompts you to save them.

Online help

Like Word, Access, PowerPoint and other Microsoft Office applications, Excel offers a searchable online help system:

- The 'help' in online help means that the information is there to assist you understand and use Excel.

- The word 'online' means that the material is presented on the computer screen rather than as a traditional printed manual.

You can search through and read online help in two ways: from the **Help** menu, or from dialog boxes.

Using Help menu options

Choose **Help | Microsoft Excel Help** or click the Online Help button on the Standard toolbar to display the three tabs of the Help Topics dialog box. These are explained on the opposite page.

 As you search through and read online help topics, you will see the following buttons at the top of the online help window:

- **Hide/Show**: Hides or displays the left pane of the online help dialog box.

- **Back/Forward**: Moves you backwards and forwards through previously visited help topics.

- **Print**: Prints the currently displayed help topic.

- **Options**: Offers a number of display choices.

Take a few minutes to look through Excel's online help
system. Remember that you will be free to use online help
during an ECDL test.

Contents tab

*This offers short
descriptions of Excel's
main features.*

*Where you see a
heading with a book
symbol, double-click
it to view the related
sub-headings.*

*Double-click on a
question mark
symbol to read the
online help text.*

Answer Wizard

*Type your question
in the box at the
top-left of the
dialog box, and
click Search.
Excel displays a list
of suggested help
topics in the lower-
left.
Click on a topic to
display the
associated text in
the right pane.*

Index tab

*Type the word or
phrase you are
interested in and
click Search.
Excel displays all
matches from the
online help in the lower
left of the dialog box.
When you find the
index entry that you
are looking for, click
on it to display the
associated text in the
right pane.*

Using help from dialog boxes

You can also access online help directly from a dialog box, as
Exercise 1.10 demonstrates.

Exercise 1.10: Using online help in a dialog box

1 Choose **View | Zoom** to display the Zoom dialog box.

2 Click on the question mark symbol near the top-right of the dialog box. Excel displays a question mark to the right of the cursor.

3 Move the mouse down and left, and click on the Page Width option.

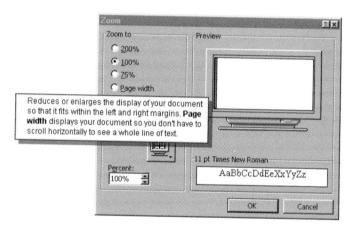

Excel displays online help text that tells you about the selected option.

Practise this exercise with other dialog boxes in Excel.

When finished, you can close your workbook and Excel. You have now completed Chapter 1 of the ECDL *Spreadsheets* module.

Chapter summary: so now you know

An Excel *workbook* is a file containing spreadsheets, which Excel calls *worksheets*. Workbook file names end in .xls.

A worksheet is made up of cells, arranged in *columns* and *rows*. Each cell has a *unique cell reference*, consisting of its column letter and row number. For example, B3 and G47.

Only one cell is the *active cell* at any one time. You make a cell active by moving the cursor to it, using the mouse, arrow keys or *name box*.

You can enter a number, text (to *label* a number), or a cell reference to any cell. Press Enter to confirm your entry. By default, Excel *left-aligns* text but *right-aligns* numbers.

To *edit* a cell, first make it editable. You do so by double-clicking it with the mouse. Alternatively, make it the active cell and then press Excel's edit key, F2.

You can *delete* the content of the active cell (but not the cell itself) by pressing Delete or Backspace.

Excel's *Undo* feature, available from a button on the Standard toolbar, allows you to reverse your recent cell entries or actions if they have produced unwanted results.

You can hide and display Excel's various *toolbars*. The two most commonly used are the Standard and Formatting toolbars.

Excel's online help system, available from the Help menu and from individual dialog boxes, provides a comprehensive and searchable guide to the program's features and procedures.

CHAPTER 2

Arithmetic with Excel

In this chapter

Prepare to be impressed. In Chapter 1 you learnt the names for the important parts of an Excel worksheet, and practised the simple operations of entering numbers, text and cell references to cells.

Now you have the basics you need to discover the power of spreadsheets in this chapter.

You will very quickly discover why people who work with numbers – such as accountants, statisticians, engineers and project managers – rely on spreadsheets to perform tedious calculations quickly, easily and accurately.

In the practical exercises you will use fewer than a dozen numbers. These simple examples differ from the multi-page financial reports of a large corporation in size only. The principles are the same. Learn the principles here in Chapter 2 and you will never meet an amount of data too large or too complex for you to master with your spreadsheet skills.

New skills

At the end of this chapter you should be able to:

- Explain what an Excel formula is, and name its components
- Use Excel formulas to add, subtract, multiply and divide numbers
- Apply the rules of arithmetic to calculations in Excel
- Recognize Excel error messages
- Use Excel's Zoom feature to enlarge and reduce the worksheet display
- Save a workbook to a diskette

New words

At the end of this chapter you should be able to explain the following terms:

- Formula
- Calculated cell
- Non-adjacent cells
- Argument
- Operator
- Constant

Formulas in Excel

I n Chapter 1 you learnt how to enter numbers, text and cell references to worksheet cells. Now it's time to discover a fourth type of cell entry, called a calculation.

To type a plus (+), hold down the Shift key and press the Equals (=) key

Calculations are the reason that you enter numbers to cells, because calculations enable you to perform arithmetic – addition, subtraction, multiplication and division – on your entered numbers.

Excel accepts two kinds of calculations: formulas and functions. This chapter shows you how to perform calculations using formulas. You will learn about functions in Chapter 3.

Formula

An equation that performs operations such as addition, subtraction, multiplication or division on data that is stored in a worksheet.

Exercise 2.1: Adding two numbers with an Excel formula

1   Open the workbook that you saved in Exercise 1.8. If cells B2 and B3 do not contain the word 'Add' and the number 1275, enter that data now.

2 Click on B4, and type the number:

25

3 Press Enter.

4 Click on B5, and type:

=B3+B4

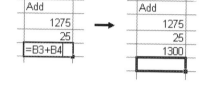

5 Press Enter.

Excel displays in B5 the sum of the contents of the two cells B3 and B4.

Congratulations! You have performed your first calculation in Excel.

Formulas and arguments

Formula and argument are two words you will meet a lot when learning about spreadsheets. So it is important that you understand what they mean.

In Exercise 2.1 the formula you used was =B3+B4. Note the following about formulas:

- Always begin formulas with the equal to (=) sign.

- Always press Enter to confirm your formula.

The components of a formula are called arguments. In the formula =B3+B4, the arguments are B3 and B4. Both are cell references. As you will see, you can also use numbers as arguments.

Argument

The inputs to a calculation that generate the result.

Next, let's perform three other arithmetic operations using Excel formulas: subtraction, multiplication and division.

Exercise 2.2: Subtracting with Excel

1 In cell D2, enter the word Subtract. (That is, type the word and press Enter.)

2 In cell D3, enter the number 1275.

3 In cell D4, enter the number 25.

4 In cell D5, enter the formula:

=D3-D4

(That is, type the formula and press Enter.)

Excel displays in D5 the result of subtracting the contents of D4 from D3.

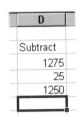

D
Subtract
1275
25
1250

Excel's Subtraction key is the Hyphen (-) key, to the left of the Equals key

Exercise 2.3: Multiplying with Excel

1 In cell F2, enter the word Multiply.

2 In cell F3, enter the number 1275.

3 In cell F4, enter the number 25.

4 In cell F5, enter the formula:

=F3*F4

Excel displays in F5 the result of multiplying the contents of F3 by F4.

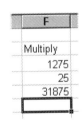

F
Multiply
1275
25
31875

Excel's Multiplication key is the Asterisk (*) key, typed by holding down the Shift key and pressing the 8 key

Exercise 2.4: Dividing with Excel

1   In cell H2, enter the word Divide.

2   In cell H3, enter the number 1275.

3   In cell H4, enter the number 25.

4   In cell H5, enter the formula:

    =H3/H4

    Excel displays in H5 the result of dividing the contents of H3 by H4.

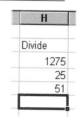

H
Divide
1275
25
51

Excel's Division key is the Forward slash (/) key, to the right of the Full stop (.) key

Calculated cells

In Exercises 2.1 to 2.4, the cells B3 and B4, D3 and D4, F3 and F4, and H3 and H4 each:

*   Contain a number, and

*   Display a number.

In other words, what they contain and what they display are the same.

Cells B5, D5, F5 and H5, however, contain one thing (a formula) but display another (a number). These are examples of calculated cells.

Calculated cell

A cell that contains a calculation but displays only the result of that calculation.

You can think of a calculated cell as an 'answer cell'.

In addition to arguments, the other type of component in a formula is the operator.

Operators

Symbols that specify the type of calculation you want to perform on the arguments of a formula. Excel's four main arithmetic operators are +, −, *, and /.

Excel offers other, more complex operators that are beyond the scope of this ECDL Spreadsheet module.

Adding down and across

Two of the most common arithmetic operations in spreadsheets are the addition of numbers that are arranged in vertical or horizontal lists. Exercises 2.5 and 2.6 provide examples of each.

Exercise 2.5: Adding a Vertical List of Numbers

1 In cells B8, B9, B10, B11 and B12, enter the numbers 1234, 4532, 5693, 3512 and 239.

2 In cell A13, enter the word:

   Total

3 In cell B13, enter the formula:

   =B8+B9+B10+B11+B12

8		1234
9		4532
10		5693
11		3512
12		239
13	Total	15210
14		

Excel displays in B13 the result of adding the specified cells.

Exercise 2.6: Adding a Horizontal List of Numbers

1 In cells B16, C16, D16, E16 and F16, enter the numbers
1234, 4532, 5693, 3512 and 239. (The same numbers
as in Exercise 2.5.)

14						
15						Total
16	1234	4532	5693	3512	239	15210
17						
18						

2 In cell G15, enter the word: Total

3 In cell G16, enter the formula:

=B16+C16+D16+E16+F16

Excel displays in G16 the result of adding the specified cells.

Adding non-adjacent cells

Excel can add cells even when they are not arranged in neat,
vertical or horizontal lists, as Exercise 2.7 demonstrates. Cells
that are not immediately adjoining one another are called
'non-adjacent cells'.

Exercise 2.7: Adding Non-Adjacent Cells

1 Enter the following numbers:

1234 in B20, 4532 in C22, 5693 in D21, 3512 in E19
and 239 in F20.

(The same numbers as in Exercises 2.5 and 2.6.)

2 In G19, enter the word Total.

3 In G20, enter the formula:

=B20+C22+D21+E19+F20

18						
19				3512		Total
20	1234				239	15210
21			5693			
22		4532				

Excel displays in G20 the result of adding the specified cells.

Non-adjacent cells

Cells that are not located immediately beside, above or below one another.

Editing formulas

In Exercise 1.5 of Chapter 1, you learnt how to edit a number in a cell. You can also edit a formula, as Exercise 2.8 demonstrates.

Exercise 2.8: Editing a Formula

1 Double-click on G20. (Alternatively, move the cursor to it with the arrow keys, and

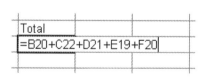

then press Excel's Edit key, F2.)

2 Using the Backspace or Delete key, delete from the formula the argument F20 and the plus operator (+) in front of it.

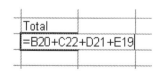

3 When finished press Enter.

Excel now displays in G20 the result of adding B20, C22, D21 and E19 only.

Combining operators

You can enter more than one type of operator in a single formula. In Exercise 2.9, you will enter formulas that contain both the addition and the subtraction operators.

Exercise 2.9: Formulas with Multiple Operators

Your company produces four products. They have fixed costs, variable costs, discounts and prices, as set out in the cells shown below.

Your task is to enter formulas to calculate the total costs for each product, and determine the profit for each product.

	A	B	C	D	E	F	G
25	Name	Fixed	Variable	Total	Discount	Price	Profit
26	Product 1	12	2		2	21	
27	Product 2	34	6		8	56	
28	Product 3	56	28		12	112	
29	Product 4	127	92		19	290	
30							

1 Enter the numbers and text in the cells as shown above.

2 Enter the formulas shown on the right in cells D26, D27, D28 and D29.

When you press Enter after typing each formula, Excel displays the calculated result.

D
Total
=B26+C26
=B27+C27
=B28+C28
=B29+C29

➡

D	
Total	
2	14
5	40
3	84
2	219

3 Enter the formulas shown on the right in cells G26, G27, G28 and G29.

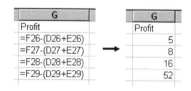

When you press Enter after typing each formula, Excel displays the calculated result as shown.

That is, the profit on each product is its price minus the sum of the total cost and the discount.

Formulas: using constants

Excel formulas can contain numbers instead of (or as well as) cell references. Excel calls these numbers 'constants'.

Constant

An argument in a formula that is a fixed number.

Here are some examples of formulas containing both cell references and constants:

26*109   =45*(A12+3)   =B2/100-B3/50

You can even enter formulas that contain only constants and no cell references, as shown in Exercise 2.10.

Exercise 2.10: Entering constant-only formulas

1 Enter the following in cell B32:

=32/4

Excel displays the result (8) in B32.

Formulas: the rules of arithmetic

Excel allows you to combine addition, subtraction, multiplication and division in a single formula. For example:

=C5*(A4+A7)-(C4/C7)

Excel follows the rules of arithmetic in calculating such formulas:

- Division first, followed by multiplication, then addition, and finally subtraction.

  For example, the following formula gives a result of 11 because Excel first multiplies 2 by 3 (resulting in 6) and then adds 5.

  =5+2*3

- You can use parentheses (brackets) to force Excel to calculate your formula in a particular order.

  For example, the following formula gives a result of 21 because Excel first adds 5 and 2 (because they are within parentheses) and then multiplies that result by 3 to give 21.

  =(5+2)*3

  Ensure that you follow every opening bracket that you type with a matching closing bracket. For example:

  6/2 * 3 + 4 = 13

  6/(2 * 3) + 4 = 5

  6/2 * (3 + 4) = 21

  6/(2 * (3 + 4)) = 0.42857

Here's a way to help you remember the order of precedence among arithmetical operators:

Oh Dear! My Aunt Sally!

Fixed factor calculations

In some calculations, you need to apply the same number or factor several times to different numbers. The fixed factor may be a currency exchange rate, for example, or an employee tax rate or sales commission rate.

It is best to place such a fixed factor in a cell of its own, and enter its cell reference as needed in formulas. Exercise 2.11 provides an example.

Exercise 2.11: Sales Commission and Tax Calculations

Your company employs four sales representatives: Edgar, Sheila, Wallace and Deirdre. In addition to a basic salary, each receives commission of 20% on goods sold. All four are taxed at a rate of 15%.

Given the information displayed below, use Excel formulas to calculate the Net Income of each employee.

	B	C	D	E	F	G	H
34							
35	Comm. Rate		0.2				
36	Tax Rate		0.15				
37							
38							
39	Person	Basic	Sales	Comm.	Gross	Tax	Net Income
40	Edgar	1200	3000				
41	Sheila	1300	3100				
42	Wallace	1600	3500				
43	Deirdre	1700	3800				

1 Enter the numbers and text in the cells as shown above. You enter 20% as .2 and 15% as .15. Excel displays your entered numbers as 0.2 and 0.15.

2 To calculate each employee's sales commission, gross income, tax payment and net income, enter the formulas as shown below.

E	F	G	H
Comm.	Gross	Tax	Net Income
=D40*D35	=C40+E40	=F40*D36	=F40-G40
=D41*D35	=C41+E41	=F41*D36	=F41-G41
=D42*D35	=C42+E42	=F42*D36	=F42-G42
=D43*D35	=C43+E43	=F43*D36	=F43-G43

3 When you press Enter after typing each formula, Excel displays the calculated result as shown below.

E	F	G	H
Comm.	Gross	Tax	Net Income
600	1800	270	1530
620	1920	288	1632
700	2300	345	1955
760	2460	369	2091

Exercise 2.12 provides an example of currency conversions, which are another type of fixed-factor type calculations.

Exercise 2.12: Currency conversion calculations

Your company sells a range of five products, priced at £100, £150, £200, £250 and £300, to the USA and Japan. The sterling-to-dollar exchange rate is 1.64, and the sterling-to-yen rate is 170.94.

Your task is to create a currency conversion table that shows the prices of your products in sterling, dollars and yen.

1 Enter the text labels and numbers as shown below.

	B	C	D
45			
46	GBP/USD	1.64	
47	GBP/JPY	170.94	
48			
49	Sterling	Dollars	Yen
50	100		
51	150		
52	200		
53	250		
54	300		

2 In cells C50 to C54, enter formulas to calculate the price of each product in dollars, obtained by multiplying its price in sterling by the exchange rate in cell C46.

In cells D50 to D54, enter formulas to calculate the price of each product in yen, obtained by multiplying its price in sterling by the exchange rate in cell C47.

Dollars	Yen
=B50*C46	=B50*C47
=B51*C46	=B51*C47
=B52*C46	=B52*C47
=B53*C46	=B53*C47
=B54*C46	=B54*C47

The formulas are as shown above right.

When you press Enter after typing each formula, Excel displays the calculated result as shown below right.

	B	C	D
45			
46	GBP/USD	1.64	
47	GBP/JPY	170.94	
48			
49	Sterling	Dollars	Yen
50	100	164	17094
51	150	246	25641
52	200	328	34188
53	250	410	42735
54	300	492	51282

Calculations and recalculations

In Exercises 2.1 to 2.12 you learnt how to use your £1,000 computer as a £10 pocket calculator! You have performed calculations using handfuls of numbers, but you can imagine how you could use the same methods to record and calculate hundreds or even thousands of numbers on a worksheet.

The power and convenience of a spreadsheet is not so much the ability to calculate as the ability to recalculate. Excel will recalculate the result of an addition (or other type of operation) whenever any of the numbers that make up the operation is changed.

Let's try it and see.

Exercise 2.13: Recalculating an addition

In Exercise 2.1 you entered the number 25 in cell B4.

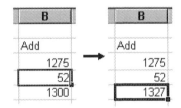

1 Click on B4, type 52, and press Enter.

Notice how Excel recalculates B5 (the 'answer cell'), and displays the new result.

Just two numbers are added in this exercise, but it could as easily have been hundreds or more.

Exercise 2.14: Recalculating a Multiplication

In Exercise 2.12 you entered a sterling-to-dollar exchange rate of 1.64 in cell C46, and a sterling-to-yen rate of 170.94 in cell C47.

1 Click on C46, type 1.68, and press Enter.

2 Click on C47, type 170.92, and press Enter.

Notice how Excel recalculates the foreign currency amounts for all five products, as shown below.

	B	C	D
45			
46	GBP/USD	1.68	
47	GBP/JPY	170.92	
48			
49	Sterling	Dollars	Yen
50	100	168	17092
51	150	252	25638
52	200	336	34184
53	250	420	42730
54	300	504	51276

To gain an appreciation of the power of spreadsheets, imagine Excel recalculating the prices for hundreds of products.

As further practice, revisit Exercise 2.11, change the commission rate (in D35), and the tax rate (in D36), and note the effect on the employees' commission, gross and net income columns.

Error messages: when bad things happen

If a formula cannot properly calculate a result, Excel displays an error message in the calculated cell indicating the type of error that has taken place. Here are the main error messages that you are likely to meet when following this ECDL module.

#####

Your cell contains a number or a calculation result that is too wide for the cell to display. This is not really an error: Excel has the correct information, it just can't display it. You will learn about adjusting column width in Chapter 3.

#VALUE!

Your formula contains text (or a cell reference that points to a cell containing text) instead of a number. Edit the formula or cell to fix the problem.

#DIV./0!

You have tried to divide a number by zero, or by a cell reference that points to a cell containing a zero.

You will see the same error message if you try to divide a number by a cell reference that points to an empty cell. Excel interprets a blank cell as containing a zero.

#REF!

Typically, your formula contains a cell reference that points to a cell that has been deleted.

Excel's Zoom views

Excel's Zoom feature enables you to magnify or reduce the worksheet display. You can use Zoom in either of two ways:

- Click in the Zoom box on the Standard toolbar, enter a number between 10 and 400, and press Enter. (You need not type the percent (%) symbol.)

- Choose the **View | Zoom** command, and select a magnification option from the Zoom dialog box.

  You can choose a preset option (25–200%), or select Custom and enter a number from 10 to 400. Alternatively, choose the Fit selection option. This magnifies or reduces the selected cell or cells so that they occupy the full screen. (You will learn about ranges of selected cells in Chapter 3.)

To return from an enlarged or reduced view to normal view, select a magnification of 100% or click the Undo button on the Standard toolbar.

Zoom and printing

The Zoom feature affects only the way that Excel displays a worksheet on screen and *not* how Excel prints a worksheet. You will learn how to print a worksheet at a size other than 100% in Chapter 3.

Saving to a diskette

Have you been saving your workbook as you went along? You should. It is also a good idea to save a copy of your workbook to a diskette. Follow the steps in Exercise 2.15 to learn how.

Exercise 2.15: Saving an Excel workbook to a diskette

1 Insert a diskette in the diskette drive of your computer:

- If it is a new diskette, ensure that it is formatted.

- If it is a previously used one, ensure that there is sufficient space on it to hold the Excel workbook file. Your workbook should be about 16KB in size.

2 Choose **File | Save As** and locate the A: drive.

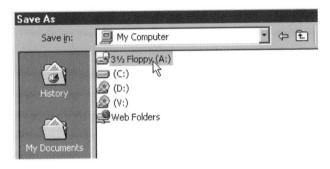

3 Excel suggests the current file name (for example, KenBloggs.xls) for you to accept or amend. Click **Save** to save the file and close the dialog box.

4 When finished, use **File | Save As** again to resave the workbook to its original location on your computer. (You will be asked if you want to replace the original file: click **OK**.)

   If you do not resave your workbook at its original location, saving the file in future (by clicking the Save button on the Standard toolbar or choosing **File | Save**) will save the workbook to the diskette and not to your computer's hard disk.

You have now completed Chapter 2 of the ECDL *Spreadsheets* module. You can close your workbook and Excel.

Chapter summary: so now you know

You can perform *calculations* on worksheet cells in two ways: using formulas and using functions. A *formula* begins with an 'equals' symbol (=) and contains one or more *operators*, for example, addition (+), subtraction (-), multiplication (*), or division (/).

The components or *arguments* of a formula can be cell references, numbers or both. A sample formula would be:

=A12+B12+3

A single formula may contain operators of different types: addition and multiplication, for example. Excel follows the rules of arithmetic in calculating formulas: division is done first, followed by multiplication, then addition, and finally subtraction. You can use parentheses (brackets) to force Excel to calculate your formula in a particular order. The following two formulas, for example, may give different results:

=(A1+A2)*B1
=A1+(A2*B1)

Excel stores the result of a calculation in a *calculated cell*, which contains the formula but displays only the calculation result.

Excel's *Zoom* feature enables you to magnify or reduce the worksheet display. Options range from 10 to 400% of normal size. Only screen display (and not printing) is affected by zooming.

If a formula cannot properly calculate a result, Excel displays an *error message* in the calculated cell indicating the type of error that has taken place.

CHAPTER 3

Functions, formatting and printing

In this chapter

Formulas, as you learnt in Chapter 2, enable you to perform calculations on numbers. In this chapter you will discover a second type of calculation method, based on functions. You will also meet the very useful AutoSum button.

When you work with numbers, it's important to get the right answers. But it's also important that your answers look good. Excel provides a wide range of formatting, alignment, border and colour features to help you give your worksheets a professional appearance. You will also learn how to change the width of columns and the height of rows.

Other topics in this chapter include adjacent and non-adjacent cell ranges, find and replace, headers and footers, and worksheet printing.

New skills

At the end of this chapter you should be able to:

- Use Excel's SUM and Average functions to perform calculations on cells, and use the AutoSum button on Excel's Standard toolbar
- Select ranges of adjacent and non-adjacent cells
- Adjust column width and row height
- Change font, font style (bold and italic), and font size
- Align cells horizontally and vertically, and rotate cells
- Apply borders and fills (coloured backgrounds to cells)
- Find, replace and spellcheck items on a worksheet
- Change page setup and insert headers and footers
- Print from Excel

New words

At the end of this chapter you should be able to explain the following terms:

- Function
- Adjacent cell range
- Non-adjacent cell range

Excel functions

You have learnt how Excel's formulas can add, subtract, multiply and divide numbers. Excel offers a second way to perform calculations: functions.

Function

A predefined formula built in to Excel and used for a specific purpose.

Most Excel functions are of interest only if you are using a spreadsheet for specialised purposes, such as statistical analysis. But two – SUM and Average – are useful to almost everyone. The SUM and Average functions are also part of the ECDL syllabus, so you need to know how to use them.

The SUM function

In Chapter 2, you learnt how to add numbers by using such formulas as:

=B3+B4+B5

You can imagine that addition formulas can become very awkward – and prone to typing errors – when they contain large numbers of arguments. For example, if there were 100 cells to add rather than just three.

- Excel's SUM function allows you to calculate the total of a vertical or horizontal list of numbers by entering just three items:

- The name of the function (in this case, SUM)

- The reference of the first cell

- The reference of the last cell

Upper- or lower-case?

As with row and column letters, you can type function names in upper- or lower-case letters. In the same way that Excel accepts A4 or a4, it accepts SUM or sum, Average or average.

In Excel's online help (and in this book), function names are written in upper-case. When entering functions on a worksheet, however, you will find it quicker to type their names in lower-case, because you need not use the Shift key.

The following exercise shows the SUM function in action.

Exercise 3.1: Using the SUM Function

1   Open the worksheet that you saved in Chapter 2.

2   Click the Sheet2 tab to display the second worksheet of the workbook.

3   In cells B3, B4 and B5, enter the numbers 2356, 4921 and 2903.

4   In cells A3, A4 and A5, enter the text Conway, Murphy and Smith to label the entered numbers.

5   Type the following function in B6 and press Enter:

6   =SUM(B3:B5)

	A	B
1		
2		
3	Conway	2356
4	Murphy	4921
5	Smith	2903
6		=sum(b3:b5)
7		

⟶

	A	B
1		
2		
3	Conway	2356
4	Murphy	4921
5	Smith	2903
6		10180
7		
8		

7   Well done! You have used Excel's SUM function to add numbers.

The AutoSum button

Because SUM is such a commonly used function, Microsoft put a button for it on the Standard toolbar.

Exercise 3.2: Using the AutoSum Button

1   Delete the SUM function, entered in Exercise 3.1, from cell B6.

2   With B6 as the active cell, click the AutoSum button on the Standard toolbar.

AutoSum button

Excel tries to 'guess' which cells you want to add together. In this example, it assumes (correctly) that the cells start at B3 and end at B5.

	A	B
1		
2		
3	Conway	2356
4	Murphy	4921
5	Smith	2903
6		=SUM(B3:B5)

3 Press Enter to confirm that B3, B4 and B5 are the cells for adding.

	A	B
1		
2		
3	Conway	2356
4	Murphy	4921
5	Sullivan	2903
6		10180
7		
8		

4 The total is displayed in cell B6.

SUM tolerates text and spaces

Excel's SUM is a tolerant function. It ignores:

- Cells containing text

- Empty cells

For example, the function =SUM(W12:W16) adds whatever numbers it finds in the cells W12, W13, W14, W15 and W16.

If any cell contains text instead of a number, or is empty, the SUM function does not display an error message. It just ignores the non-numeric cells and continues on adding up the numeric ones.

In the next exercise you will enter more numbers and text to your worksheet, Sheet2.

Exercise 3.1: Entering more numbers and text

1   On Sheet2, enter two further columns of numbers in columns C and D, as shown below. Across the top of columns B, C, D and E, enter a row of labels (text), also as shown below.

(The month of March is omitted deliberately. You will insert a new column for March in Exercise 4.2 of Chapter 4.)

	A	B	C	D	E
1					
2		January	February	April	Total
3	Conway	2356	3621	4560	
4	Murphy	4921	4055	3542	
5	Smith	2903	3308	3622	

2   Use the AutoSum button to total the numbers in rows 3, 4 and 5. In E3 enter =SUM(B3:D3), in E4 =SUM(B4:D4) and in E5 =SUM(B5:D5).

When you click on E5 and then click the AutoSum button, Excel will 'guess' which cells you want to total. Excel assumes (incorrectly) that they are the two immediately above it, E3 and E4, as shown.

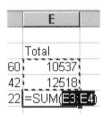

When this happens, double-click on E5 (or press F2) to make the cell editable. Next, change the arguments of the SUM function to =SUM(B5:D5).

3   Use the AutoSum button to total, in row 6, the numbers in each of the columns C, D and E. In C6, enter =SUM(C3:C5), in D6 =SUM(D3:D5) and in E6 =SUM(E3:E5).

Your worksheet should now look as shown below.

	A	B	C	D	E
1					
2		January	February	April	Total
3	Conway	2356	3621	4560	10537
4	Murphy	4921	4055	3542	12518
5	Smith	2903	3308	3622	9833
6		10180	10984	11724	32888
7					

The Average function

This Excel function – you guessed it – finds the average of a group of numbers.

As with the SUM function, the Average function begins with the = sign. Then follows the function name, and finally the arguments within parentheses. Exercise 3.2 provides an example of the Average function in use.

Exercise 3.2: Using the Average function

1 Click the Sheet1 tab to display the first worksheet in your workbook.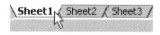

2 In cell B44 enter the label Average.

3 In cell C44 enter the following formula:

=AVERAGE(C40:C43)

4 C44 now displays the average value of the contents of cells C40, C41, C42 and C43.

5   Repeat step 3 for columns D, E, F, G and H to average the cells immediately above them.

Row 44 should now look as shown.

| 44 | Average | 1450 | 3350 | 670 | 2120 | 318 | 1802 |

Formatting and aligning single cells

Formatting refers to the *appearance* of numbers and text in cells. It includes such actions as making cell content bolder (heavier) and putting it in italics.

The *position* of numbers and text within cells is called alignment. Three common options are left, centred and right. The quickest way to apply a formatting or alignment option to a cell is to select it and then click the relevant button on Excel's Formatting toolbar.

Format buttons

Alignment buttons

You now learn how to format and align cells on a worksheet – in this case, Sheet2 of your workbook.

Exercise 3.3: Formatting and aligning cells

1   On Sheet2 of your worksheet, click on cell B2.

2   Click the Bold button on the Formatting toolbar. Excel displays the word January in bold.

3   Click the Centre-align button on the Formatting toolbar. Excel centre-aligns the word January.

4   Click on cell A3, and then click the Italic button on the Formatting toolbar. Excel displays the word Conway in italics.

Formatting and aligning cell groups

You can save time and mouse-clicks by formatting or aligning a group of cells in one, single operation. Before you can do so, you must first select the group of cells.

You can select a group of cells by clicking on the top-left cell in the group, and then dragging the mouse across the other cells. Exercise 3.4 shows you how.

Exercise 3.4: Formatting and aligning a cell range

1   Click cell C2.

2		January	February	April	Total
3	Conway	2356	3621	4560	10537

2   Drag the mouse across to cell E2.

2		January	February	April	Total
3	Conway	2356	3621	4560	10537

3   Click the Bold button on the Formatting toolbar.

4   Click the Centre-align button on the Formatting toolbar.

5   Select cell A4.

6   Drag the mouse down to cell A5.

7   Click the Italic button on the Formatting toolbar.

Sheet2 should now look as shown below.

	A	B	C	D	E
1					
2		January	February	April	Total
3	Conway	2356	3621	4560	10537
4	Murphy	4921	4055	3542	12518
5	Smith	2903	3308	3622	9833
6		10180	10984	11724	32888

Click anywhere on the worksheet outside the selected cells A4 and A5 to deselect the two cells.

Cancelling a selection

Finished formatting your selected cells? Or selected the wrong cells? To cancel a selection, click anywhere outside the selected cell or range.

Cancelling a selection does not delete the cell or range from the worksheet. It just deselects the selected cells.

Cell ranges

In Excel, a group of cells in a worksheet is known as a cell range.

Cell range

A group of cells on a worksheet.

Cell ranges are of two kinds: adjacent and non-adjacent.

Adjacent cell range

A group of cells that are directly beside, above or below one another. Adjacent cells are sometimes called contiguous cells.

You identify an adjacent cell range by:

- The cell reference of the top-left cell

- A colon (:)

- The cell reference of the bottom-right cell

For example, the adjacent cell range A1:B2 includes the following four cells: A1, A2, B1 and B2.

Adjacent cell ranges may also include cells in one column only (for example, B2:B5) or in one row only (for example, D9:F9).

Non-adjacent cell range

Can you select cells that are located on different parts of a worksheet as a single range? Yes. This is what Excel calls a non-adjacent cell range.

Non-adjacent cell range

A group of cells that are not directly beside, or above or below, one another. Also called non-contiguous cells.

A non-adjacent cell range can consist of individual cells dotted around the worksheet. Or, as in Exercise 3.5, it can contain a number of smaller, sub-groups of adjacent cells.

You select a non-adjacent cell range by selecting the first cell (or first sub-group of adjacent cells), holding down the Ctrl key, and then selecting further cells (or adjacent ranges).

A non-adjacent cell range is written with commas to separate the individual cells (for example, A2, B3, C4) or the smaller, sub-groups of adjacent cells (for example, A2:A6, H4:H8).

Exercise 3.5: Selecting a non-adjacent cell range

1 Select the first cell or sub-group of adjacent cells. For example, B2:B6 (that is, cells B2, B3, B4, B5 and B6).

	A	B	C	D	E
1					
2		January	February	April	Total
3	Conway	2356	3621	4560	10537
4	Murphy	4921	4055	3542	12518
5	Smith	2903	3308	3622	9833
6		10180	10984	11724	32888

2 Hold down the Ctrl key.

3 Select the next cell or next sub-group of adjacent cells. For example, cell range E2:E6.

	A	B	C	D	E
1					
2		January	February	April	Total
3	Conway	2356	3621	4560	10537
4	Murphy	4921	4055	3542	12518
5	Smith	2903	3308	3622	9833
6		10180	10984	11724	32888

You can continue this process until you have selected all the cells in the non-adjacent range that you want to select.

Click anywhere outside the cell range to cancel the selection.

Selected cells and the active cell

In Chapter 1 you learnt how to select a single cell – by clicking on it with the mouse, moving the cursor to it with the arrow keys, or entering its cell reference in the name box. That cell is then the active cell.

So, for a single cell, the terms 'active cell' and 'selected cell' mean the same thing. And 'Select a cell' is simply another way of saying 'Make a cell the active cell'.

While you can select any number of cells at one time, only one cell can be the active cell. Excel displays selected cells in reverse (white text on black background). The active cell is shown as black text on a white background.

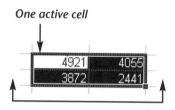

One active cell

Four selected cells

F8: Excel's Select key

In Exercise 3.4 you selected an adjacent cell range by selecting the first cell, and then dragging the mouse across the other cells in the range.

An alternative method is to select the first cell, press F8, and then press the arrow keys to extend the selected area over the other cells. F8 is Excel's Select key. You may find this method faster than using the mouse, but you can use it only for selecting adjacent cell ranges.

Selecting columns and rows

Excel offers quick ways of selecting one or more rows
or columns.

- To select an entire row, click on the row heading.

- To select several adjacent rows, click the heading of the
  top or bottom one, and hold down the mouse button
  as you drag down or up.

- To select several non-adjacent rows, click the heading
  of the first, hold down the Ctrl key, and click on the
  other headings.

- To select an entire column, click on the
  column heading.

- To select several adjacent columns, click
  on the heading of the first or last, and
  then drag with the mouse to the right
  or left.

- To select several non-adjacent columns, click on the
  heading of the first, hold down the Ctrl key, and click
  on the headings of the others.

Deleting rows and column contents

To delete the contents of one or a selection of rows or columns,
select the rows or columns, and press the Delete key.

This operation removes only the row or column cell contents, leaving behind empty rows or columns. It does not delete the actual rows or columns. You will learn how to remove rows and columns from worksheets in Chapter 4.

Selecting the entire worksheet

To select the whole worksheet, click on the top-left of the worksheet, where the row heading meets the column heading.

A fast way to delete the contents of all cells on a worksheet is to select the entire worksheet, and then press Delete.

Adjusting column width and row height

You can change the appearance of your worksheet by adjusting the width of one or more columns, or the height of one or more rows.

- **Column width**: To change the width of a column, move the mouse to the column heading, and then drag the boundary on the right side of the column heading until the column is the width you want. See Exercise 3.6.

- **Row height**: To change row height, move the mouse to the row heading, and then drag the boundary below the row heading until the row is the height you want. See Exercise 3.7.

Exercise 3.6: Adjusting column width

1   In the column heading of Sheet2, click on the boundary
    line between columns A and B.

	A	B	C	D	E
1					
2		January	February	April	Total
3	Conway	2356	3621	4560	10537

2   Drag the boundary to the left, making column A narrower.

←

	A	B	C	D	E
1					
2		January	February	April	Total
3	Conw	2356	3621	4560	10537

3   Reverse the effect of step 2 by dragging the column A
    boundary to the right, so restoring column A to its
    original width.

Exercise 3.7: Adjusting row height

1   In the row heading, click on the
    boundary between rows 2 and 3.

2   Drag the line down about one
    centimetre until it looks like that shown below.

    Well done. You have changed the height of a row on
    your worksheet.

	A	B	C	D	E
1					
2		January	February	April	Total
3	Conway	2356	3621	4560	10537

Leave the row at its increased height for Exercise 3.8.

Vertical alignment

The three alignment buttons (left, centre and right) on the Formatting toolbar enable you to position cell contents horizontally (left-to-right). Excel also allows you to align cell contents vertically (top-to-bottom). Exercise 3.8 provides an example of vertical alignment.

Exercise 3.8: Changing vertical alignment

1   Select cell range B2:E2 in row 2, whose height you increased in Exercise 3.7.

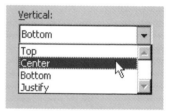

2   Choose **Format | Cells**, select the Alignment tab, select the Center option from the Vertical: list, and click **OK**.

Excel now aligns the cells' content vertically so that it is centred between the top and bottom of each cell's boundaries.

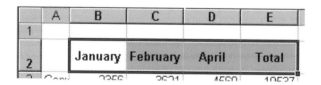

3   Click once on the Undo button on the Standard toolbar to return the cells to the default vertical alignment of Bottom, and then click a second time to return the row to its original, normal height.

Orientation

Another Excel formatting feature is the ability to rotate or 'orient' the text or numbers to a specified angle within a cell. See Exercise 3.9.

Exercise 3.9: Rotating cell content

1   Select cell range B2:E2, choose **Format | Cells**, select the Alignment tab, type 90 in the Degrees box, and click OK.

Excel now rotates the cells' content so that it is positioned at ninety degrees to the horizontal, as shown below.

	A	B	C	D	E
1					
2		January	February	April	Total

2   Click the Undo button on the Standard toolbar to return the cells' orientation to the default value of zero degrees.

Entering a positive number in the Degree box rotates the cell content in the anti-clockwise direction. A negative number of degrees rotates the cell content in the clockwise direction.

Fonts

A font (also called typeface) is a particular style of text. What fonts are installed on your computer? Click the arrow on the drop-down Font box on Excel's Formatting toolbar to see.

Viewing the fonts on your computer

There are really just two kinds (families) of fonts: serif and sans serif. Sans serif just means without serifs. You can recognize which family a font belongs to by asking: Do its characters have serifs (tails or squiggles) at their edges?

A serif font

A sans serif font

Excel's default font is Arial, a sans serif font. The most commonly used serif font is Times New Roman. Arial and other sans serif fonts are usually better for displaying numbers. You may want to use a serif font for worksheet labels.

Font

A typeface: a particular style or text. The two main font families are serif and sans serif.

You can change the font of any cell or cell range by first selecting the cells and then choosing a new font from the drop-down list on the Formatting toolbar.

Font sizes

Font size is measured in a non-metric unit called the point, with approximately 72 points equal to one inch. Excel's default font is 10 point.

You can change the font size of any cell or cell range by first selecting the cells, and then choosing a new font size from the drop-down list on the Formatting toolbar.

Font colours

You can change the colour of cell contents from Excel's default of Automatic. What colour is Automatic? Automatic is black, unless the cell background is black or another dark colour, in which case Automatic switches to white.

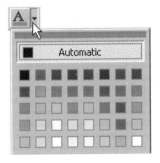

You can change the colour of the text or number displayed in any cell or cell range by first selecting the cells, clicking the arrow on the right of the Font Color button on the formatting toolbar, and then clicking on a colour.

In the next exercise you will practise changing the fonts, font sizes and colours of the labels in Sheet1 of your workbook.

Exercise 3.10: Changing fonts, font sizes and colours

1 Click the Sheet1 tab to display the first worksheet of your workbook.

2 Click cell B2. Hold down the Ctrl key and click also on the following cells: D2, F2 and H2.

3 From the Formatting toolbar, change the font to Times New Roman, the font size to 12 point, and the font colour to dark blue. Next, click on the Bold and Center-align buttons.

Your worksheet should now look as follows.

Add		Subtract		Multiply		Divide	
1275		1275		1275		1275	
52		25		25		25	
1327		1250		31875		51	

Cell borders

Excel provides a wide choice of borders that you can use to highlight a particular cell or cell range – such as cells containing sub- and final totals on a worksheet. You can access these options by clicking the arrow on the right of the Borders button on the Formatting toolbar.

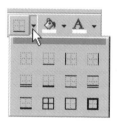

The most commonly used cell border options are the single bottom line (the default), the double and heavier bottom lines, and the outline. The last places a border on all four sides of the selected cells. Exercise 3.11 provides an example.

Exercise 3.11: Placing a bottom border on cells

1   Select the non-adjacent cells B4, D4, F4 and H4.

2   Click the arrow on the right of the Borders button, and, from the list of options displayed, click the heavy, single bottom line.

Your worksheet should now look as shown.

Add	Subtract	Multiply	Divide
1275	1275	1275	1275
52	25	25	25
1327	1250	31875	51

Cell colour backgrounds

As with cell borders, Excel allows you to change the background colour of a cell – what Excel calls the Fill Color.

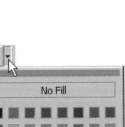

You access this option by clicking the arrow on the right of the Fill Color button on the Formatting toolbar.

Exercise 3.12 provides an example.

Exercise 3.12: Changing the Fill Color

1   Select the adjacent cell range A25:G25.

2   Click the arrow on the right of the Fill Color button, and click the Yellow button.

Your worksheet should now look as shown.

Name	Fixed	Variable	Total	Discount	Price	Profit
Product 1	12	2	14	2	21	5
Product 2	34	6	40	8	56	8
Product 3	56	28	84	12	112	16
Product 4	127	92	219	19	290	52

In Exercise 3.13 you will further practise your cell border and fill colour skills.

Exercise 3.13: Further cell border and colour practice

1 Select the adjacent cell range A25:G29.

2 Click the arrow on the right of the Borders button, and click the outline (all four cell edges) border type.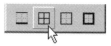

3 Select cell range B35:D36.

4 Click the arrow on the right of the Borders button, and click the hollow outline (edges only) border type.

5 Select cell range D35:D36.

6 Click the arrow on the right of the Borders button, and click the left-edge border type.

7 Select cell range B43:H43.

8 Click the arrow on the right of the Borders button, and click the heavy bottom line border type.

9 Select non-adjacent cell range B46:C47, B49:D54.

10 Click the arrow on the right of the Borders button, and click the outline (all four cell edges) border type.

11 With the non-adjacent cell range still selected, click the arrow on the right of the Fill Colors button, and click the Gray (25%) option.

Finding cell content

You can search a worksheet for label text, numbers that were entered directly, numbers resulting from calculations, and calculation components (function names, cell references, arithmetic operators and constants) as follows:

- Select the range of cells you want to search. (To search the whole worksheet, click any cell.)

- Choose **Edit | Find**.

- In the Find what: box, enter the item you want to find, and select **Find Next**.

You can cancel a Find operation in progress by pressing the Esc key.

Find options

Excel's Find feature offers the following options:

- **Search**: Select the direction you want to search in: down through columns, or rightwards across rows.

- **Look In**: The type of cells you want to search through.

- **Match Case**: Searches only for characters that match the case of the entered search text. For example, a search for 'smith' does not find 'Smith'.

- **Find Entire Cells Only**: Searches only for complete matches. For example, a search for 'Sm' does not find 'Smith', and 330 does not find 3308.

Replacing cell content

Anything that you can search for in a worksheet with **Edit | Find**, you can replace with a specified alternative. For example, you could replace occurrences of cell reference F34 with F36. The procedure is as follows:

- Select the relevant range of cells. (To perform the find-and-replace operation on the whole worksheet, click any cell.)

- Choose **Edit | Replace**.

- In the Find what: box, enter the item you want to replace. In the Replace with: box, enter the replacement item. (You can delete from the selected cells the characters in the Find what: box by leaving the Replace with: box blank.)

- Select **Find Next**. To replace only the highlighted occurrence of the found characters, select **Replace**.

- To replace *all* occurrences of the found characters in the selected cells, click **Replace All**.

Exercise 3.14 provides an example of Excel's Find-and-Replace feature.

Exercise 3.14: Finding and replacing text on a worksheet

1 Click the Sheet2 tab to display the second worksheet of your workbook.

2 Select the cell range A2:E6.

3 Choose **Edit | Replace**. In the Find what: box, type Smith. In the Replace with: box, type Sullivan.

4 Select the 'Match case' and 'Find entire cells only' options. Select **Replace All**.

Replace	? X
Fi_n_d what:	
Smith	Find Next
Re_p_lace with:	
Sullivan	Close
_S_earch: By Rows ▼ ☑ Match _c_ase	_R_eplace
☑ Find entire cells _o_nly	Replace A_l_l

5 Sheet2 should now look as shown below.

	A	B	C	D	E
1					
2		January	February	April	Total
3	Conway	2356	3621	4560	10537
4	Murphy	4921	4055	3542	12518
5	Sullivan	2903	3308	3622	9833
6		10180	10984	11724	32888
7					

Spellchecking

Excel can check the spelling of text on all or part of a worksheet. To check your spelling, follow this procedure:

- Select the range of cells whose spelling you want to check. To check the whole worksheet, click any cell.

Spelling button

- Click the Spelling button on Excel's Standard toolbar.

When Excel meets a word that it does not recognize from its spelling dictionary (the same dictionary used by Microsoft Word), it displays the Spelling dialog box, as shown below.

The following are your main options:

- **Ignore**: Leave this occurrence of the word unchanged.

- **Ignore All**: Leave this and all other occurrences of the word in the selected cells unchanged.

- **Change**: Correct this occurrence of the word, but prompt again on further occurrences.

- **Change All**: Correct this occurrence of the word – and all other occurrences without further prompting.

- **Add**: Add the word to the custom (your personal) dictionary. Use this option for the names of people or places, or abbreviations or acronyms, that you type regularly. Excel will recognize such added words during future spellchecks of any worksheet.

Practise by spellchecking Sheet1 and Sheet2 of your workbook.

Page setup

In the remainder of this chapter you will learn about Excel's various printing options, beginning with those available on the four tabs of the **File | Page Setup** dialog box: the Page, Margins, Header/Footer, and Sheet tabs.

Paper size

Located on the Page tab of the **File | Page Setup** dialog box, this option allows you to select the size of the paper you want to print on. The default is A4, the European standard paper size (21 cm wide and 29.7 cm high).

Orientation

Also on the Page tab, you can select the orientation or the direction in which the page is printed. Your options are Portrait ('standing up') and Landscape ('on its side').

Scaling

Two scaling options on the Page tab enable you to reduce or enlarge the worksheet printout:

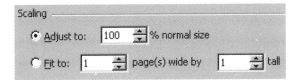

- **Adjust to:** You can enter a number in the range 10–400% of normal size. (You need not type the % symbol.)

- **Fit to:** Reduces the worksheet (or selected cells) so that it fits on the specified number of pages. You can specify the number of pages vertically (tall), horizontally (wide), or both.

Margins

The margins are the distance that the printed worksheet or selected cells are positioned in from the four edges of the printed page. You set them on the Margins tab of the **File | Page Setup** dialog box. You can specify separate margins for headers and footers, which are covered in the next topic.

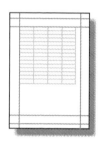

It is unlikely that you will need to change Excel's default margin values – top and bottom, 2.5 cm, left and right, 1.9 cm.

The Margins tab also allows you to centre your worksheet or selected cells horizontally (positioned evenly between the left and right margins of the printed page), vertically (between the top and bottom margins), or both.

Gridlines and headings

By default, Excel does not include cell boundary lines or row and column headings on printouts. You can change either or both of these settings on the Sheet tab of the **File | Page Setup** dialog box.

Headers and footers

Headers and footers are pieces of text that appear at the top and bottom of every page of a printed worksheet. Typically, they contain such details as file name, author name, date and page number.

With Excel, you need only type in header and/or footer text once, and the program repeats the text on every page. You can apply formatting – font, bold and italics – to text in the headers and footers.

Here are a few facts about headers and footers in Excel:

- You insert them with the Header/Footer tab of the **File | Page Setup** command.

- The Header/Footer tab offers a drop-down list of suggested header and footer texts, from which you can choose the one that best suits your needs.

- You can edit and/or format your chosen header or footer text by clicking the Custom header or Custom footer button on the Header/Footer tab, and then selecting the required options.

- The Custom buttons enable you to format the header or footer text, and insert any or all of the following items: page number, total number of pages, date, time, Excel file name and worksheet name.

- When setting header and footer margins on the Margins tab of the **File | Page Setup** dialog box, ensure that the values are less than the top and bottom page margins – otherwise, the header and footer text may overlap the cells on the printout.

Exercise 3.15 provides an example of Excel's header and footer feature in action.

Exercise 3.15: Inserting a header and footer

1 With Sheet1 of your workbook selected, choose **File | Page Setup** and select the Header/Footer tab.

2 On the Header drop-down list, select the Excel workbook file name – in this case, KenBloggs.xls.

3 On the Footer drop-down list, select Page 1 of ?.

KenBloggs.xls

Header:

| KenBloggs.xls | ▼ |

[Custom Header...]   [Custom Footer...]

Footer:

| Page 1 of ? | ▼ |

Page 1 of 1

---

4 Click the Custom Header button, select the file name in the Center section, click the Text Formatting button, and make the file name bold.

Text formatting button

5 In the Left section, type My First Workbook. In the Right section, type ECDL Module 4.

Left section:	Center section:	Right section:
My First Workbook	**KenBloggs.xls**	ECDL Module 4

6   Click **OK** to return to the Header/Footer tab of
     the Page Setup dialog box.

Date button

7   Click the Custom footer button, click in the
     Left section, and then click the Date button.

8   Click in the Right section, and then click
     the Time button.

Time button

Left section:	Center section:	Right section:
&[Date]	Page &[Page] of &[Pages]	&[Time]

9   Click **OK** to return to the Header/Footer tab of the Page
     Setup dialog box. Click **OK** again to close the dialog box.

     Well done. You have inserted a header and footer in
     your workbook. You cannot see headers and footers on
     screen; they appear on printouts only.

Printing options

Excel offers a wide range of printing options. These include
the ability to preview a worksheet on your screen before you
print it, and the choice of printing all your worksheet,
selected cells or pages, or your entire workbook.

Page Break Preview

Select **View | Page Break Preview** to see where page breaks will occur when you print your spreadsheet. You can change the position of page breaks by dragging the dividing lines to new positions. Excel will resize the data to fit on the page. Select **View | Normal** to return to the normal workbook view.

Print Preview

This displays each page as it will appear when it is printed on paper. To preview your worksheet, choose **File | Print Preview**. Alternatively, click the Print Preview button on the Standard toolbar.
Click **Close** to return to your worksheet.

Print Preview button

Print range options

When you choose **File | Print**, you have the following options regarding which parts of your workbook you may print:

- **All**: The current worksheet.

- **Pages**: To print one or a range of pages from the current worksheet, enter the page number(s) here.

- **Selection**: Prints only the currently selected cells on the current worksheet.

- **Entire Workbook**: All worksheets that contain data in the workbook.

Other options on the Print dialog box allow you to specify how many copies you want to print, and whether you want the pages collated or not.

Exercise 3.16: Printing a worksheet

1   Click the Sheet1 tab to select the first worksheet of your workbook.

2   Choose **File | Print**, accept the default options, and click **OK**.

3   Your printout should look like that shown.

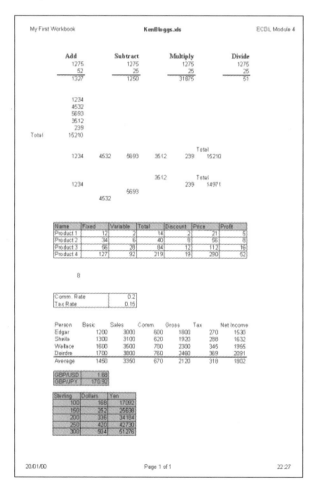

Save and close your workbook and Excel. You have now completed Chapter 3 of the ECDL *Spreadsheets* module.

Chapter summary: so now you know

Functions are predefined formulas built into Excel that allow you to perform specific calculations. As with formulas, functions always begin with an equal to (=) symbol.

With the *SUM* function, you need enter only two arguments when totalling a vertical or horizontal list of cells: the first and last cell references. An example of a SUM function would be:

=SUM(A2:A6)

A fast way to total a vertical or horizontal list of cells is to select them and click the *AutoSum* button. Excel tries to 'guess' which cells you want to add. If Excel has guessed correctly, just press Enter to confirm the suggested arguments. If not, edit the arguments of the SUM function.

The *Average* function, as its name suggests, calculates the average of a vertical or horizontal list of numbers. For example:

=AVERAGE(D5:F5)

A *cell range* is a group of cells on a worksheet. You can *select* an *adjacent* cell range by dragging the mouse across it. Select a *non-adjacent* cell range by selecting the first cell (or first sub-group of adjacent cells) and then holding down the Ctrl key when selecting further cells (or adjacent ranges).

Selected cells can be *formatted* (bold or italic), *aligned* (horizontally or vertically), and *rotated*. You can also add *borders* and *fills* (coloured backgrounds), and change *fonts* and *sizes*.

You can adjust *column width* and *row height* by dragging the cell boundaries in the row and column headings.

You can *search* all or part of a worksheet for label text, entered numbers, numbers resulting from calculations, and calculation components (function names, cell references, arithmetic operators and constants). And you can *replace* found items with alternatives. You can also *spell-check* all or part of a worksheet.

The standard page size is A4, and pages can be oriented in *portrait* or *landscape*. A *margin* is the distance of the cells from a particular edge of the page.

Headers and *footers* are small text items that occur on every printed page, and typically contain such details as the workbook name, author name and date. Either can also contain the automatically generated *page number.*

Excel's *print options* include a Print Preview feature and the ability to print selected cells only.

CHAPTER 4

Inserting, sorting and moving cells

In this chapter

Excel users spend only part of their time creating new workbooks and entering and formatting data in the worksheet cells. The remainder is spent reopening existing workbooks and amending previously entered data.

In this chapter you will learn how to perform three types of maintenance tasks.

Row and column insertion allows you to position new cells within a worksheet area that already contains cells with data in them. Insertion (or deletion) means that surrounding cells must adjust their position to make way for the new data (or fill the spaces previously occupied by the deleted data).

Copying, cutting and pasting enable you to reproduce or move cells within the same worksheet, between worksheets in the same workbook, or between different workbooks. By copying and cutting calculations you will find out about relative and absolute cell references.

Finally, sorting allows you to rearrange selected cells in a sequence different from that in which they were entered to the worksheet.

New skills

At the end of this chapter you should be able to:
- Insert and delete rows, columns and cells
- Copy, cut and paste the contents of cells
- Explain the difference between relative and absolute cell references, and identify calculations in which absolute cell references are appropriate
- Sort cells according to one or two criteria
- Insert symbols and special characters from Word to Excel.

New words

At the end of this chapter you should be able to explain the following terms:
- Marquee
- Relative cell reference
- Absolute cell reference
- Sort
- Sort order

Inserting and deleting rows

With over four million cells on a single worksheet, why would you want to add some more? Answer: sometimes you need to insert a row or column to hold new data *within* a range of cells that already contains text and numbers.

Exercises 4.1 and 4.2 take you through the steps of inserting new rows and columns.

Exercise 4.1: Inserting a new row

1 Open the second worksheet of your workbook, Sheet2.

2 Select the heading of the row immediately below where you want to insert the new row. For example, to insert a new row below row 4, click on the heading of row 5.

	A	B	C	D	E
1					
2		January	February	April	Total
3	Conway	2356	3621	4560	10537
4	Murphy	4921	4055	3542	12518
5	Sullivan	2903	3308	3622	9833
6		10180	10984	11724	32888

3 Choose **Insert | Rows**. Excel inserts a new row of blank cells.

	A	B	C	D	E
1					
2		January	February	April	Total
3	Conway	2356	3621	4560	10537
4	Murphy	4921	4055	3542	12518
5					
6	Sullivan	2903	3308	3622	9833
7		10180	10984	11724	32888

4   Enter new text and numbers in cells A5, B5, C5 and D5, as shown on the next page. Excel recalculates the totals on row 7 automatically as you add the new numbers.

5   In cell E5, enter the following SUM function to add the cells of row 5:

=SUM(B5:D5)

Excel recalculates E7, the total of the Totals column, to include E5, the sum of the numbers that you have entered in row 5. Your worksheet should look as shown.

	A	B	C	D	E
1					
2		January	February	April	Total
3	Conway	2356	3621	4560	10537
4	Murphy	4921	4055	3542	12518
5	Smith	3872	2441	4949	11262
6	Sullivan	2903	3308	3622	9833
7		14052	13425	16673	44150
8					

6   To make your worksheet more readable, insert a blank row above the column totals, as shown.

	A	B	C	D	E
1					
2		January	February	April	Total
3	Conway	2356	3621	4560	10537
4	Murphy	4921	4055	3542	12518
5	Smith	3872	2441	4949	11262
6	Sullivan	2903	3308	3622	9833
7					
8		14052	13425	16673	44150

Deleting rows

To delete a row, select the row heading and choose **Edit |
Delete**. The row beneath moves up to fill the space previously
occupied by the deleted row.

Inserting and deleting columns

Inserting a new column in a worksheet is similar to inserting
a new row. Exercise 4.2 shows you how.

Exercise 4.2: Inserting a new column

1   Select the heading of the column
    immediately to the right of where you
    want to insert the new column.

    For example, to insert a new column to
    the right of column D, click on the
    heading of column E.

2   Choose **Insert | Columns**. Excel inserts a
    new column of blank cells.

3 Enter new text and numbers in D2:D6 as shown on the next page.

Excel recalculates the totals in column F automatically as you add the new numbers in column D.

4 To total the new numbers in column D, enter the following function in cell D8:

=SUM(D3:D6)

	A	B	C	D	E	F
1						
2		January	February	March	April	Total
3	Conway	2356	3621	4185	4560	14722
4	Murphy	4921	4055	3814	3542	16332
5	Smith	3872	2441	2888	4949	14150
6	Sullivan	2903	3308	3487	3622	13320
7						
8		14052	13425	14374	16673	58524

5 To make your worksheet more readable, insert a column to the right of the April column.

6 This blank column is wider than it needs to be. In the column heading, click on the boundary between columns F and G, and then drag the boundary to the left.

E	F	G		E	F	G
April		Total		April		Total
4560		14722		4560		14722

Deleting columns

To delete a column, select its heading and choose **Edit | Delete**. The column to the right moves left and fills the space previously occupied by the deleted column.

Inserting and deleting cells

You can insert individual cells
on a worksheet by first selecting
a cell immediately below or to
the right of where you want to
insert the new cell, and then
choosing **Insert | Cells**.

To delete a cell, select it and
choose **Edit | Delete**.

Be careful about inserting or
deleting a new cell or cell range, because Excel adjusts the
position of the surrounding cells accordingly. Excel prompts
you, when inserting, to choose whether the surrounding cells
should move right or down, and, when deleting, whether
they should move left or up.

Copying and pasting cell contents

Suppose you have text or a number in one cell, and you want
to copy it to another cell. How do you do it? Of the many
ways of copying and pasting a cell or cells on a worksheet,
here are the two most convenient:

- Drag-and-drop

- Right-clicking

You will learn about each method in Exercises 4.3 and 4.4.

Exercise 4:3: Copy and paste with drag-and-drop

1   Select the cell you want to copy from.

2   For example, click the Sheet1 tab
    to display your first worksheet.
    Type 1234 in cell B57 and press
    Enter. Next, click B57 to select it.

    See how the cursor is shaped like a plus sign (+).

3   Move the cursor to the bottom
    edge of the selected cell and
    hold down the Ctrl key. Excel
    changes the cursor from a plus
    sign to an arrow with a smaller plus sign.

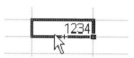

    (You can move the cursor to any edge of the selected
    cell – it doesn't matter which edge. The cursor still
    changes shape.)

4   Holding down the Ctrl key, drag the cell to the destination
    cell that you want to paste to – for example, D57.

5   Release the mouse button first, and then the Ctrl key.

    (If you release Ctrl first, Excel cuts rather than copies the
    cell contents.)

    If there is already something in cell D57, Excel
    overwrites it with the pasted data.

    Well done. You have copied a number from one cell of a
    worksheet to another – without clicking a toolbar
    button or choosing a menu command!

Exercise 4:4: Copy and paste by right-clicking

1 Select the cell whose contents you
   want to copy. As in Exercise 4.3,
   select B57.

2 Right-click with the mouse.

3 Choose **Copy** from the pop-up
   menu. Excel places the contents of B57 in the clipboard.

4 Click cell F57.

5 Right-click with the mouse.

6 Choose **Paste**.

   If there is already something in cell F57, Excel overwrites
   it with the pasted data.

You are not limited to using drag-and-drop and right-clicking
with single cells only. You can use both methods with
selected ranges of cells.

About the clipboard

When you copy (or cut) and paste by any means other than
drag-and-drop, the copied (or cut) cells are held in a
temporary storage area called the clipboard. Here are seven
points you should remember about the clipboard:

- The clipboard is temporary. Turn off your computer
  and the clipboard contents are deleted.

- The same clipboard is available to all Windows
  applications. For example, you can copy from
  PowerPoint and paste into Excel.

- The clipboard can hold up to *twelve* copied items at a time. When you copy the second and subsequent items, Excel displays the Clipboard toolbar. (If it doesn't appear, choose **View | Toolbars | Clipboard** to display it.)

Clipboard toolbar

- Each copied item is added to the clipboard, and stored in the next available space. What happens if you attempt to copy a thirteenth item? Excel responds by asking if you want to overwrite the oldest of the twelve items currently in the clipboard.

- If you rest the cursor over an item's icon on the Clipboard toolbar, Excel displays a descriptive label about the item.

- To paste the most recently copied item from the clipboard, click the Paste button on the Standard toolbar, or choose **Edit | Paste**. To paste a different item, click its icon on the Clipboard toolbar. To paste all previously copied items (Excel calls this 'Collect and Paste'), click the Paste All button on the Clipboard toolbar.

- An item stays in the clipboard after you paste from it, so you can paste the same item to as many locations as you need.

The flashing marquee

When you copy (or cut) a cell or cell range by any means other than drag-and-drop, Excel surrounds the selected cells with a flashing rectangle called a marquee.

Marquee

A flashing rectangle that Excel uses to surround a cell, or cell range, that you have copied to the clipboard.

You can remove a marquee at any stage by pressing the Esc key at the top-left of your keyboard.

If you remove a marquee, Excel removes the contents of the selected cell or cell range from the clipboard.

Exercise 4.5: Copy and paste a cell range

In this exercise you will copy and paste an adjacent cell range. You will use the keyboard shortcuts to perform the copy and paste actions.

1   Type 1234 in cells B57, C57, D57 and E57.

2   Select the cell range B57:F57.

3   Press Ctrl+c to copy the cells to the clipboard.

4   Click cell B59, and press Ctrl+v to paste from the clipboard.

Excel copies the cells to the new cell range B59:F59, as shown below.

	B	C	D	E	F
56					
57	1234	1234	1234	1234	1234
58					
59	1234	1234	1234	1234	1234
60					

You can paste from the clipboard to several locations in a single action, as Exercise 4.6 demonstrates.

Exercise 4.6: Copy and paste to multiple locations

1   With cell range B57:F57 still in the clipboard from Exercise 4.5, select the adjacent cell range B61:F64.

2   Press Ctrl+v to paste to the cells. All four adjacent rows of the destination cell range now contain the pasted cells.

3   Select the non-adjacent cell range B66:F66, B68:F68, B70:F70.

4   Press Ctrl+v to paste to the cells. The three non-adjacent rows of the destination cell range now contain the pasted cells.

    Your worksheet should look as shown.

	B	C	D	E	F	G
60						
61	1234	1234	1234	1234	1234	
62	1234	1234	1234	1234	1234	
63	1234	1234	1234	1234	1234	
64	1234	1234	1234	1234	1234	
65						
66	1234	1234	1234	1234	1234	
67						
68	1234	1234	1234	1234	1234	
69						
70	1234	1234	1234	1234	1234	
71						

Pasted to an adjacent cell → rows 61–64

Pasted to a non-adjacent cell → rows 66, 68, 70

Cutting and pasting cell contents

Cut and paste differs from copy and paste in that cutting removes the content of the original cells, whereas the contents of copied cells remain in their original location.

Cutting does not remove the cells, in the way that the **Edit |**
Delete command does. It just removes their contents, leaving
behind empty cells.

To cut and paste using drag-and-drop, do not hold
down the Ctrl key while dragging the cell
contents to their new location.

Copy button

To cut and paste using the pop-up menu, choose
Cut rather than **Copy**. The keyboard shortcut for
cutting a cell or cell range is Ctrl+x. **Cut, Copy**   *Cut button*
and **Paste** commands are also available on
Excel's **Edit** menu.

Yet another cut or copy and paste method
is to use the relevant buttons on Excel's   *Paste button*
Standard toolbar.

Copying between worksheets and workbooks

You are not limited to copying or cutting and pasting cells
within the same worksheet (such as Sheet1). You can also
copy or cut and paste between different worksheets of the
same workbook (such as Sheet1 and Sheet2 of your
workbook), and even between different workbooks.

Exercise 4.7: Copying and pasting between workbooks

1   On Sheet2, select cell range A2:G8.

2   Choose **Edit | Copy** to copy the cells to the clipboard.

3   Click the New button on the Standard toolbar to
    open a new workbook. The new workbook
    opens with Sheet1 displayed.

New button

4   In the name box of the new workbook,
    type A100 and press Enter. This moves the cursor to cell
    A100, making it the active cell.

5   Choose **Edit | Paste** to paste the cell range from
    the clipboard.

    You have completed the exercise. Close the new
    workbook without saving it.

Moving calculations

Numbers and text can be copied or cut and pasted without
problems. But what about calculations? Can errors arise when
moving formulas or functions?

   Yes – but only when fixed-factor calculations are involved.
As you learnt in Chapter 2, these are calculations where a
common cell reference, indicating the fixed factor, is used in
formulas or functions on different rows or columns.
Common examples of fixed factors are currency exchange
rates, and tax and sales commission rates.

   Exercise 4.8 demonstrates the problem that can arise when
copying fixed-factor calculations.

Exercise 4.8: Copying fixed-factor calculations

1   On Sheet1, select the cell range B46:D54, and press
    Ctrl+c to copy it to the clipboard.

2   Click cell F46, and press Ctrl+v. Excel copies the cells to their new location without error.

For example, C50 contains the formula =B50*C46. The corresponding cell in the pasted data, G50, contains the formula =F50*G46.

If you click on any calculated cell you can see that Excel has automatically adjusted the formula arguments to reflect the new cell references.

3   Select the cell range B49:D54, and press Ctrl+c to copy it to the clipboard.

4   Select cell J49, and press Ctrl+v to paste from the clipboard.

This time the pasting of the cells does produce calculation errors. Excel has changed the cell references of the two fixed factors (the dollar and yen conversion rates) so that the formula cells now 'point to' the new cell locations K46 and K47 – but these cells are empty.

	J	K	L
46			
47			
48			
49	Sterling	Dollars	Yen
50	100	=J50*K46	=J50*K47
51	150	=J51*K46	=J51*K47
52	200	=J52*K46	=J52*K47
53	250	=J53*K46	=J53*K47
54	300	=J54*K46	=J54*K47
55			

There is a way to remedy this problem. First, select the pasted cell range J49:L54, and delete it with the **Edit | Clear | All** command. This removes both the cell content and the cell formatting.

5   Double-click on C50, and change the formula to the following: B50*C46. Similarly, in C51:C54, change all references from C46 to C46.

Next, in cells D50:D54, change all cell references from C47 to the new format of C47. Your worksheet formulas should now look as shown below.

49	Sterling	Dollars	Yen
50	100	=B50*C46	=B50*C47
51	150	=B51*C46	=B51*C47
52	200	=B52*C46	=B52*C47
53	250	=B53*C46	=B53*C47
54	300	=B54*C46	=B54*C47

6 Select cells B49:D54, and press Ctrl+c to copy them.

7 Select cell J49, and press Ctrl+v to paste from the clipboard. No errors! If you click on any of the formula cells, you can see that Excel has not adjusted the cell references that contained the $ symbol. Although pasted to a new location, the calculations continue 'pointing to' the original cell references of the two currency conversion rates.

In this exercise you have learnt the difference between relative and absolute cell address. The next topic provides further details.

Cell references: the two kinds

In Chapter 1 you learnt that each cell on a worksheet has a unique reference, written in the form A1 – column letter first, row number second.

In fact, Excel supports two kinds of cell references: relative (the A1 type you know already) and absolute (the A1 type you met in Exercise 4.8).

Why is one type of cell reference not enough? The answer, as you discovered in Exercise 4.8, lies in the way that Excel copies and pastes calculations that contain cell references.

A cell reference that Excel adjusts automatically when the calculation cell containing it is moved to a new location is called a relative cell reference.

Relative cell reference

A reference to a cell or cell range in the format A1. Excel changes a relative cell reference when you copy or move a formula or function containing such a reference to a new location.

An absolute cell reference, however, does not change when the calculation containing it is moved to a new location. Accordingly, you should use absolute cell references when entering fixed factor type calculations. You can make part of a cell reference absolute and part relative. For example, G$13 or $D17.

Absolute cell reference

A reference to a cell or cell range in the format A1. Excel does not adjust an absolute cell reference when you copy or move a calculations containing such a reference.

Exercise 4.9: Working with absolute cell references

In this Exercise you will use the Find and Replace feature to convert relative cell references to absolute ones, and then copy the related calculations to a new location.

1 On Sheet1, select cell range E40:E43.

2 Choose **Edit | Replace**. Type the values shown below, and select **Replace All**.

Replace ? ✕

Find what:
D35

Replace with:
D35

Search: By Rows ▾   ☐ Match case
☐ Find entire cells only

Find Next
Close
Replace
Replace All

3 Select cell range G40:G43, and repeat step 2. This time, replace all occurrences of D36 with D36.

You are now ready to copy the cells that 'point to' the two fixed factors: sales commission and taxation rate.

4 Select cell range B39:H44, and press Ctrl+c to copy them to the clipboard.

5 Click cell J39, and press Ctrl+v. The calculations copy without error.

Sorting: reordering cells by content

The order in which you typed entries in a worksheet may not be the order in which, later on, you would prefer to display or print that information. Suppose, for example, that you have entered a list of numbers in a column of a worksheet.

By selecting the cell range and choosing the Sort Ascending (or Sort Descending) button, you can rearrange the cells so that Excel displays them in order of increasing (or decreasing) value. The reordered list may now be easier to read than the original, unsorted one.

Sorting

Rearranging columns of cells based on the values in the cells. Sorting does not change the content of cells, only their location.

Excel offers a number of sequencing options, called sort orders.

Sort order

A particular way of ordering cells based on value. A sort order can be alphabetic or numeric, and can be in ascending (0 to 9, A to Z) or descending (Z to A, 9 to 0) sequence.

Exercise 4.10: A simple Sort

1 On Sheet1, click B73 and enter the label Original.

2 In the six cells immediately below B73, type the following vertical list of numbers: 453, 123, 340, 683, 987 and 213.

3 In cells C73 and D73, enter the labels Ascending and Descending.

4 Select the cell range B74:B79, and press Ctrl+c.

5 Select the cell range C74:D79, and press Ctrl+v.

6 Select the cell range C74:C79, and click the Sort Ascending button on the Standard toolbar.

Sort Ascending button

7 Select the cell range D74:D79, and click the Sort Descending button on the Standard toolbar.

Your worksheet should look as shown.

Sort Descending button

	B	C	D
72			
73	Original	Ascending	Descending
74	453	123	987
75	123	213	683
76	340	340	453
77	683	453	340
78	987	683	213
79	213	987	123

The two sort buttons give you a quick, one-click way of reordering a cell range. As you will discover in Exercise 4.11, Excel's **Data | Sort** menu command provides an additional option: you can sort a cell range based on the values in more than a single column. This is called a multiple sort.

Exercise 4.11: A multiple Sort

The rows of Sheet2 are currently arranged in alphabetic sort order according to surname: Conway first, then Murphy, Smith and, lastly, Sullivan.

	A	B	C	D	E	F
1						
2		January	February	March	April	Total
3	Conway	2356	3621	4185	4560	14722
4	Murphy	4921	4055	3814	3542	16332
5	Smith	3872	2441	2888	4949	14150
6	Sullivan	2903	3308	3487	3622	13320
7						
8		14052	13425	14374	16673	58524

1   Select row 7 by clicking on its row heading, and choose **Insert | Rows**. Next, press Ctrl+y twice. This is the keyboard shortcut for Excel's Repeat command. Excel inserts three new, blank rows under row 6.

	A	B	C	D	E	F	G
6	Sullivan	2903	3308	3487	3622		13320
7							
8							
9							
10							
11		14052	13425	14374	16673		58524

2 Enter in rows 7, 8 and 9 the text and numbers as shown.

	A	B	C	D	E	F	G
1							
2		January	February	March	April		Totals
3	Conway	2356	3621	4185	4560		14722
4	Murphy	4921	4055	3814	3542		16332
5	Smith	3872	2441	2888	4949		14150
6	Sullivan	2903	3308	3487	3622		13320
7	Rafferty	2512	2864	3290	3741		12407
8	Higgins	3463	3981	4210	4974		16628
9	Smith	5951	6226	6481	6852		25510
10							
11		25978	26496	28355	32240		113069

In row 11, edit the arguments of the SUM functions to include the three new rows. For example, in B11 enter the function =SUM(B3:B9).

Enter new SUM functions in G7, G8 and G9 to calculate the row totals. For example, in G8 enter =SUM(B8:E8).

3 Select column B by clicking on its column heading, and choose the **Insert | Columns** command. In the new column, enter the first names as shown.

	A	B	C	D	E	F	G	H
1								
2			January	February	March	April		Total
3	Conway	John	2356	3621	4185	4560		14722
4	Murphy	Robert	4921	4055	3814	3542		16332
5	Smith	Zowie	3872	2441	2888	4949		14150
6	Sullivan	Andrew	2903	3308	3487	3622		13320
7	Rafferty	Aidan	2512	2864	3290	3741		12407
8	Higgins	Tracey	3463	3981	4210	4974		16628
9	Smith	Catherine	5951	6226	6481	6852		25510
10								
11			25978	26496	28355	32240		113069

4 Select cell range A3:H9, and choose **Data** | **Sort**.

By default, Excel shows the first column in the selected range, column A, in the Sort by: drop-down box.

In the Then by: drop-down box, select Column B.

Next, select the sort order of Ascending for both columns A and B, and click **OK**.

Your worksheet should now resemble that shown.

	A	B	C	D	E	F	G	H
1								
2			January	February	March	April		Total
3	Conway	John	2356	3621	4185	4560		14722
4	Higgins	Tracey	3463	3981	4210	4974		16628
5	Murphy	Robert	4921	4055	3814	3542		16332
6	Rafferty	Aidan	2512	2864	3290	3741		12407
7	Smith	Catherine	5951	6226	6481	6852		25510
8	Smith	Zowie	3872	2441	2888	4949		14150
9	Sullivan	Andrew	2903	3308	3487	3622		13320
10								
11			25978	26496	28355	32240		113069

The multiple-column sort is useful where one column has duplicate entries. In this exercise, cells A5 and A9 both initially contained the same text entry of 'Smith'.

Symbols and special characters

If you have completed the ECDL Word Processing module, you will know that Microsoft Word allows you to insert symbols and special characters in your documents.

- **Symbols**: Among these are foreign language letters with accents (such as á, é, ä, and ë), fractions, and characters used in science and mathematics.

- **Special Characters**: These include copyright (©), registered (®) and trademark (™) symbols, plus typographic characters such as the en (or short) dash, the em (or long) dash, and various types of opening and closing quotes.

Unlike Word, Excel offers no command for inserting symbols or special characters. As Exercise 4.12 shows, however, you can paste symbols and characters from Word to Excel.

Exercise 4.12: Inserting a special character and symbol to a worksheet

1 On Sheet1 of your workbook, type 100C in B82.

2 Start Microsoft Word. It should open with a new, blank document ready for you to type into.

3   Choose **Insert | Symbol**, select the Symbols tab, and double-click the degree character (°). Click **Close** to close the dialog box.

4   Select the degree character (°) in the Word document, and press Ctrl+c. You can now close the Word document and Word itself. You need not save the document.

5   Switch to Excel, double-click cell B82 to make it editable, position the cursor between the 100 and the C, and press Ctrl+v.

100°C

6   Cell B82 should now look as shown.

Chapter summary: so now you know

A common maintenance task in Excel is *row and column insertion*. Insertion results in the surrounding cells adjusting their positions to make way for the new data.

Conversely, *row and column deletion* causes the surrounding cells to move up or to the left, to fill the spaces previously occupied by the deleted data. You can also insert and delete individual cells and cell ranges.

You can reproduce (copy) or move (cut) a selected cell or cell range within the same worksheet, between worksheets in the same workbook, or between different workbooks. A wide variety of *copy*, *cut* and *paste* methods are provided by Excel, including drag-and-drop, commands on the pop-up menu activated by right-clicking, menu-bar commands, keyboard shortcuts, and buttons on the Standard toolbar.

Excel automatically adjusts the cell references in calculations whenever the calculations are pasted to a new location. To prevent Excel from adjusting a cell reference in this way, specify the cell address as an *absolute cell reference* in the format A1. Absolute cell references are most commonly used with fixed-factor type calculations.

Sorting allows you to rearrange selected cells on the basis of the values they contain. Sorting changes only the location of cells, and not their content. The *sort order*, the particular way in which cells are arranged by value, can be alphabetic or numeric, and can be in ascending (0–9, A–Z) or descending sequence (Z–A, 9–0).

You cannot insert symbols and special characters in Excel directly, but you can insert them in a Word document, and then copy or cut and paste them from Word to Excel.

CHAPTER 5

More about numbers, text and calculations

In this chapter

In Chapters 1 and 2 you learnt the basics of working with numbers, cell references and text. Now it's time to build on what you know.

Here you will discover that there are really four types of number and two types of cell reference, and that Excel treats the different types in different ways.

You will also learn more about entering text, and meet AutoFill, a convenient, time-saving feature for entering data in cells.

New skills

At the end of this chapter you should be able to:
- Choose the appropriate number format for the type of numbers that you want to enter and store in your worksheet
- Enter text across multiple columns
- Enter numbers as text
- Recognize the type of numbers that should be entered in calculations as absolute rather than relative cell references
- Use AutoFill to copy numbers and text, and to increment number series and special entries (dates, days, months and years)
- Use AutoFill to copy calculations that apply to multiple rows or columns

New words

At the end of this chapter you should be able to explain the following terms:
- Number format
- Comma style
- Percent style
- Absolute cell reference
- AutoFill
- General format
- Currency style
- Relative cell reference
- Increment

Numbers: the different formats

In Chapter 1 you learnt that a number was one of the four kinds of entries you could type in a worksheet cell – the others were text, cell references, and calculations (formulas and functions).

In fact, Excel recognises many types of numbers, and calls each a number format. Do not confuse this term with the use of the word format for stylistic items such as bold and italic.

Number format affects only the way that a number looks on screen and on printouts – and not its value. Consider the following example:

- A cell contains the number 1.2345.

- The same cell has a number format of one decimal place.

The number will display as 1.2. But when its cell is used in calculations, the value used will be 1.2345. This can lead to surprising results on occasion!

	A	B	C
1	1.2345	2	2.469
2	1.2	2	2.469

In the example on the right, cell A1 is multiplied by B1, and cell A2 by B2. The results are shown in C1 and C2. A1 contains the same value as A2, but is formatted with only one number after the decimal point.

Number format

The way in which Excel displays a number on screen and on printouts. Number format affects only the appearence and not the value of numbers.

The General format

Excel's default number format is called the General format. Unless you change to a different number format, Excel applies this format to every number you enter.

123.4
345.75
9383.5
45

Here are some things you need to know about the General format.

Trailing zeros after the decimal point

A zero you enter as the last digit after a decimal point is called a trailing zero. The General format does not display trailing zeros.

Enter 123.00, for example, and Excel's General format displays 123. Enter 123.40, and Excel's General format displays 123.4.

Thousands separators

The General format does not automatically insert the comma symbol (,) to separate thousands.

Enter 2500, for example, and Excel displays it as 2500, not 2,500.

Currency symbols

If you type a currency symbol (such as £) before a number (such as 123), Excel may treat your entry as text rather than a number. As a result, using the entry of £123 in a calculation may generate Excel's #VALUE! error message. Alternatively, Excel may simply ignore your entry when performing the calculation.

Unsuitable for financial amounts

All the above points make the General format unsuitable for displaying amounts of money on a worksheet.

The Comma style

Change to the Comma style for Excel to insert a comma to separate thousands. Excel also displays all numbers to two places of decimals. Exercise 5.1 demonstrates the Comma style.

Comma Style button

Exercise 5.1: Changing number format to the Comma style

1   Open Sheet2 of your workbook and select cell range C3:C9.

2   Click on the Comma Style button on the Standard toolbar.

C
January
2356
3463
4921
2512
5951
3872
2903

→

C
January
2,356.00
3,463.00
4,921.00
2,512.00
5,951.00
3,872.00
2,903.00

Excel inserts commas and two places of decimals in the selected cell range, as shown on the right.

3   Choose **Edit | Undo Style** (or press Ctrl+z) to revert to General format.

The Currency style

Change to the Currency style when your numbers represent amounts of money. Exercise 5.2 demonstrates the Currency style.

Exercise 5.2: Changing number format to the Currency style

1   On your worksheet select cell range C3:H11.

2   Click on the Currency Style button on the Standard toolbar.

Currency Style

Excel inserts the currency symbol (£), the thousands separator (,) and two places of decimals (including, where necessary, trailing zeros).

button

	C	D	E	F	G	H
1						
2	January	February	March	April		Total
3	£ 2,356.00	£ 3,621.00	£ 4,185.00	£ 4,560.00		£ 14,722.00
4	£ 3,463.00	£ 3,981.00	£ 4,210.00	£ 4,974.00		£ 16,628.00
5	£ 4,921.00	£ 4,055.00	£ 3,814.00	£ 3,542.00		£ 16,332.00
6	£ 2,512.00	£ 2,864.00	£ 3,290.00	£ 3,741.00		£ 12,407.00
7	£ 5,951.00	£ 6,226.00	£ 6,481.00	£ 6,852.00		£ 25,510.00
8	£ 3,872.00	£ 2,441.00	£ 2,888.00	£ 4,949.00		£ 14,150.00
9	£ 2,903.00	£ 3,308.00	£ 3,487.00	£ 3,622.00		£ 13,320.00
10						
11	£25,978.00	£26,496.00	£28,355.00	£32,240.00		£113,069.00

The Percent style

This number format performs two actions. It:

- Multiplies the selected cell or range by 100.

- Places the percent sign (%) after each selected number.

Use it to display decimal fractions (such as 0.0525) as more readable percentages (such as 5.25%).

In Exercise 5.3 you will generate some decimal fractions suitable for expression as percentages. In Exercise 5.4 you will then change the numbers to the Percent style.

Exercise 5.3: Creating decimal fractions

In this exercise you will add two new items to Sheet2:

- A new column to show each person's total as a proportion of the overall total

- A new row to show each month's total as a proportion of the overall total

1 Enter the percent symbol (%) in cells I2 and B13, and make the symbols bold and centre-align them.

2 In I3, enter the formula =H3/H11 to calculate the proportion of the total contributed by John Conway.

I
%
0.130204
0.147061
0.144443
0.109729
0.225614
0.125145
0.117804

Enter similar formulas for cells I4:I9.

For example, in I5 enter = H5/H11 and in I6 enter =H6/H11. Column I should look as shown.

3 In C13 enter the formula =C11/H11 to calculate the proportion of the total contributed in January.

4 Enter similar formulas for cells D13:F13. For example, to D13 enter = D11/H11. Row 13 should look as shown below.

	B	C	D	E	F
12					
13	%	0.22975351	0.23433479	0.25077607	0.28513563

Exercise 5.4: Applying the Percent style

Now you will display the calculation results from Exercise 5.3 as percentages, using the Percent style. You will also apply a fill (coloured background) to the percentage cells.

Percent Style
button

1 Select range I3:I9 and click the Percent Style button. Also centre-align the cells.

2 With range I3:I9 still selected, click the drop-down arrow to the right of the Fill Color button on the Formatting toolbar.

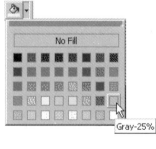

3 From the colour palette, choose Gray-25%. Click **OK**.

4 Repeat steps 1, 2 and 3 for C13:F13.

	C	D	E	F	G	H	I	
1								
2	January	February	March	April		Total	%	
3	£2,356.00	£3,621.00	£4,185.00	£4,560.00		£14,722.00	13%	
4	£3,463.00	£3,981.00	£4,210.00	£4,974.00		£16,628.00	15%	
5	£4,921.00	£4,055.00	£3,814.00	£3,542.00		£16,332.00	14%	
6	£2,512.00	£2,864.00	£3,290.00	£3,741.00		£12,407.00	11%	
7	£5,951.00	£6,226.00	£6,481.00	£6,852.00		£25,510.00	23%	
8	£3,872.00	£2,441.00	£2,888.00	£4,949.00		£14,150.00	13%	
9	£2,903.00	£3,308.00	£3,487.00	£3,622.00		£13,320.00	12%	
10								
11	£25,978.00	£26,496.00	£28,355.00	£32,240.00		£113,069.00		
12								
13	23%	23%	25%	29%				
14								

Well done. You have finished this exercise. Your
worksheet should now look as shown above.

Changing from the General format

There are two ways that you can change Excel's number format:

• First enter the numbers, and then change the
number format.

• Change the number format of the blank cells first, and
then enter the numbers.

The second method is better. If you are creating a new
worksheet to enter financial amounts, select the whole
worksheet and change the number format to Currency style
before entering any numbers. The Currency style will affect
only numbers you enter, and not any text entries.

The Number format

Spreadsheets are often used to record physical measurements and the results of laboratory experiments. Such numbers do not represent financial amounts, so the Currency style is inappropriate. Moreover, such numbers typically require a number of decimal places greater than two or three. The number format to apply in such situations is called ... Number format. Exercise 5.5 provides an example.

Exercise 5.5: Specifying the number of decimal places

Your task is to record the following numbers to four places of decimals: 3.4512, 5.13, 9.59383 and 4.531.

1   Click the Sheet1 tab to display the first worksheet of your workbook.

2   Select cell range B84:B88 and choose **Format | Cells**.

3   On the Number tab, select the Category of Number, and select 4 for Decimal places.

4   Click on B84, and enter the first number. Next, enter the remaining numbers in the other three cells in the range.

As shown here, Excel displays your cell entries to the specified number of decimal places.

3.4512
5.1300
9.5938
4.5310

- Where an entered number has more than four decimal places, Excel rounds up or down to four

- Where the number has fewer, Excel adds trailing zeros

Also available on the Number tab of the **Format | Cells** dialog box is the option to specify the thousands separator (,).

☐ U̲se 1000 Separator (,)

Toolbar buttons

Two buttons on Excel's Formatting toolbar offer quick ways of increasing or reducing the number of decimal places displayed in a selected cell or range. Each time you click on a button, the number of decimal places in the selected cells is increased or decreased by one.

Increase Decimal button

Decrease Decimal button

The buttons work with numbers in the General, Currency and Number formats.

Excel and dates

Whether entered with financial transactions or results of experiments, dates can be very important in a worksheet. Excel treats dates as numbers, with the serial number one corresponding to the date January 1, 1900. In this way Excel can add and subtract dates, and include them in other calculations.

Entering dates

Use a slash or a hyphen to separate the parts of a date.
For example:

17/10/85

26-Nov-90

If you type in just the day and the month, for example 13/02 or 19-11, Excel assumes the current year.

When you type a date that Microsoft Excel recognizes, it applies one of its built-in date formats to the cell, and right-aligns it.

If Microsoft Excel cannot recognize the date, the date is recorded as text, and is left-aligned in the cell.

Formatting dates

The way that Excel displays entered dates depends on the number format applied to the cell containing the dates.

To view a list of possible date options, choose **Format | Cells**, select the Number tab, and select Date in the Category: list. You can then see the date format options in the Type: list. Become familiar with how Excel handles dates by entering a number of dates in different formats in your worksheet. Then, select the cells and apply to your entries some of the formats listed in the **Format | Cells** dialog box.

```
┌─────────────────────────────────────────────────────┐
│ Format Cells                                  ? ✕     │
├─────────────────────────────────────────────────────┤
│  Number │ Alignment │ Font │ Border │ Patterns │ Protection │
│                                                       │
│  Category:               ┌Sample────────────────────┐│
│  ┌──────────────┐        │ workingworldmr@furturejhb.co.za ││
│  │General      ▲│        └──────────────────────────┘│
│  │Number       │                                      │
│  │Currency     │        Type:                         │
│  │Accounting   │        ┌────────────────────────┐   │
│  │Date         │        │3/14                   ▲│   │
│  │Time         │        │3/14/98                 │   │
│  │Percentage   │        │03/14/98                │   │
│  │Fraction     │        │14-Mar                  │   │
│  │Scientific   │        │14-Mar-98               │   │
│  │Text         │        │14-Mar-98               │   │
│  │Special      │        │Mar-98                  │   │
│  │Custom      ▼│        │March-98               ▼│   │
│  └──────────────┘        └────────────────────────┘   │
│                                                       │
│  Date formats display date and time serial numbers as date values. Use Time │
│  formats to display just the time portion.            │
│                                                       │
│                              ┌────────┐  ┌────────┐   │
│                              │   OK   │  │ Cancel │   │
│                              └────────┘  └────────┘   │
└─────────────────────────────────────────────────────┘
```

Regional Settings

Options you select in the Regional Settings of the Windows Control Panel affect both the currency and date conventions applied by Excel to your cell entries:

- **Changing currency**: To use a different currency in your workbooks, choose **Start | Settings | Control Panel**, and double-click on the Regional Settings icon. On the Regional Settings tab, select the required country. On the Currency tab, accept or amend the currency conventions such as symbol, number of decimal places, and digit-grouping symbol.

Regional Settings

- **Changing date**: To use the date conventions of another country in your workbooks, select the required country on the Regional Settings tab, and, on the Date tab, accept or amend the calendar conventions.

Excel and text

Two further items you need to know about Excel and text: you can enter text that displays across several columns of a worksheet, and you can enter numbers as text.

Text across multiple columns

Sometimes you may want to enter a line of text that is longer than the width of a single cell. Excel allows you to do this – provided that the text does not run into any cell that has data in it.

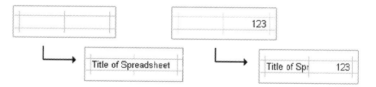

Exercise 5.6 provides an example of entering and displaying text that stretches across several columns.

Exercise 5.6: Entering text across multiple columns

1   Select row 1 of Sheet2 by clicking on the row heading.

2   Choose **Insert | Rows**.

3   Press Ctrl+y to repeat the row insertion. You now have two new, blank rows at the top of the worksheet.

4   In C2, enter the following text:

First Quarter Sales Figures for 2001

5   Select C2, click on the Font Size drop-down box, and select 14 point.

With C2 still selected, click on the Bold and Italic buttons on the Formatting toolbar.

The top rows of Sheet2 should now look as shown.

	A	B	C	D	E	F	G	H	
1									
2			*First Quarter Sales Figures for 2001*						
3									

Entering numbers as text

Why would you ever want Excel to treat a number as anything other than a number? The answer is when the number is not an amount to be used in a calculation but an identifier of some kind. Examples include part and model numbers (such as 010-34 or M5339), ID numbers (such as 99-10837), and telephone and fax numbers.

If you find it hard to think of a telephone number as anything other than a number, imagine how ridiculous it would be to add two telephone numbers together!

To enter a number as text, you must first apply the Text format to the empty cells, and then enter the numbers, as shown in Exercise 5.7. If you enter the numbers first, Excel will not apply the Text format to them and you will need to reenter all the numbers!

Exercise 5.7: Formatting numbers as text

1 On Sheet2, select cells B20:B23.

2 Choose **Format | Cells**.

3 On the Number tab, select Text from the Category list, and click **OK**.

4 Enter the numbers in cells B20:B23 as shown here.

5 Excel treats the numbers as text. You can now delete the four entries from the worksheet.

010-56
M56-47N
091-10000
W1-S9

Excel's AutoFill feature

Excel provides a very convenient feature called AutoFill for copying or incrementing (increasing in a defined sequence) the entries in a cell or range.

Exercise 5.8: Using AutoFill to copy and increment numbers and text

1 In Sheet1, enter the following in cell range B19:F19, C20.

19		12	12	Hello	Jan	Mon
20			13			

2 Click on cell B19 and position the cursor over the fill handle – the black square at the bottom-right of the selected cell.

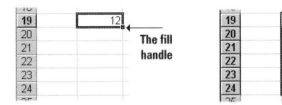

3   Drag the fill handle down to cell B24. Excel copies the contents of cell B19 to the other selected cells.

4   Select cell range C19:C20 and drag the fill handle down to C24.

5   Select D19 and drag the fill handle down to D24.

6   Select E19 and drag the fill handle down to E24.

7   Select F19 and drag the fill handle down to F24.

Your worksheet should now look as shown.

19	12	12	Hello	Jan	Mon
20	12	13	Hello	Feb	Tue
21	12	14	Hello	Mar	Wed
22	12	15	Hello	Apr	Thu
23	12	16	Hello	May	Fri
24	12	17	Hello	Jun	Sat

AutoFill and single numbers and text

For cell ranges B19:B24 and D19:D24, you began by selecting a single cell containing a number (12) and text item (Hello). As you dragged the fill handle, Excel copied the number and text into the cells that you dragged over.

AutoFill and number series

For cell range C19:C24 you began by selecting two cells. Excel recognized that they contained two numbers in an increasing series (12 and 13). As you dragged the fill handle, Excel placed increments of the series (14, 15 and so on) into the cells that you dragged over.

AutoFill and months, days, times and years

For cell ranges E19:E24 and F19:F24 Excel recognized that the single cell you selected contained the name of a month and a day. As you dragged the fill handle, Excel placed increments of the series (Feb, Mar ... and Tue, Wed, ...) into the cells below.

Excel also recognizes times (such as 9:00 or 12:30), dates (such as 1-May or 10-April) and years (such as 1996 or 2001).

AutoFill and calculations

Columns or rows of a worksheet often need the same action applied to them; for example, summing or averaging. Use AutoFill in a two-step process to avoid entering calculations (formulas and functions) individually to sum or average each row or column.

- Enter the calculation for one row or column.

- Use AutoFill to copy the formula or function to the adjacent cells.

AutoFill and cell references

AutoFill adjusts the cell references as it copies the calculation to the selected cells.

Where a calculation contains a fixed factor – such as a tax, currency conversion or sales commission rate – you will *not* want Excel to adjust the fixed factor's cell reference as it AutoFills the selected cells. In such cases, first change the fixed factor's cell reference to an absolute cell reference. Exercise 5.9 shows AutoFill used with relative and absolute cell references.

Exercise 5.9: Using AutoFill to copy calculations

1   On Sheet2, select cell range H6:I11, and press Delete to delete its contents.

Cell I5 now shows 100%, and the total cell H13 shows £14,722.00.

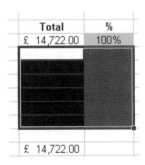

2   Select cell H5 and drag the fill handle down to cell H11.

AutoFill extends the calculation in H5 to the cells in the range H6:H11.

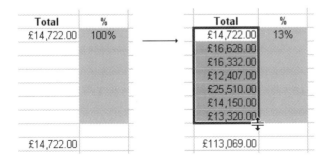

In each case, AutoFill adjusts the cell reference. For example, cell H5 contains the function =SUM(C5:F5) but cell H9 contains the function =SUM(C9:F9).

3 Select cell I5, and edit the function to change relative cell reference H13 to absolute cell reference HI3.

4 With I5 still selected, drag the fill handle down to cell I11.

AutoFill extends the calculation in I5 to the cells in the range I6:I11. As it does this AutoFill adjusts the relative cell reference H5 but not the absolute cell reference HI3.

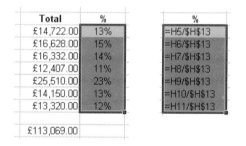

AutoFill works across rows as well as down columns, as you will learn in steps 5 and 6 of this exercise.

5 Select cell range D13:F13, and press Delete to delete their contents.

6 Select C13 and drag the fill handle to the right as far as cell F13.

£25,978.00 £26,496.00 £28,355.00 £32,240.00   £113,069.00

AutoFill keyboard shortcuts

You may find it quicker to apply AutoFill using the keyboard shortcuts rather than by dragging the fill handle with the mouse. Follow these steps:

- Select the cells you want to fill from.

- Drag the mouse down (or right) to select the cells you want to fill.

- Press Ctrl+d to fill down or Ctrl+r to fill right.

AutoFill

> *An Excel tool for quickly copying or incrementing (increasing in a defined sequence) the entries in a cell or range.*

You have now finished Chapter 5 of the ECDL *Spreadsheets* module. You may save and close your workbook, and close Excel.

Chapter summary: so now you know

Excel's default number format, the *General format*, does not display trailing zeros, does not automatically insert commas to separate thousands, and is unsuitable for entering financial amounts. The *Comma style* automatically inserts a comma to separate thousands, and displays all numbers to two places of decimals.

The *Currency style* automatically inserts your national currency symbol, and follows your currency's convention for decimal places.

The *Percent style* multiplies numbers by 100, and places the percent sign (%) after each one.

When changing to a non-default number format, it is better to do so *before* you enter your numbers. Only numbers and not text are affected by number formatting.

You can enter *multi-column* text (provided all the cells used are blank) and format *text as numbers*. This can be useful when the numbers are identifiers (part numbers, phone numbers and so on) rather than amounts.

In calculations, cells can have *relative references* or *absolute references*. Excel changes relative cell references when you copy or move the calculation to another cell; absolute references are unchanged by copying or moving. Use absolute cell references for cells containing fixed factors such as tax rates.

AutoFill copies the contents of a cell to other, selected cells in the same row or column. AutoFill can also increment a series of numbers, times, dates, days, months and years.

CHAPTER 6

Charting with Excel

In this chapter

So far you have used Excel to enter, edit, calculate, format and re-position cells on your worksheets.

In this chapter you will learn how to present the contents of your worksheet cells in what Excel – an American product – calls a chart. On this side of the Atlantic, we would use the term 'graph' or 'diagram' rather than chart.

New skills

At the end of this chapter you should be able to:
• Use Excel's Chart Wizard to create charts that are based on the numbers, text and calculations in your worksheet
• Choose the appropriate options from the dialog boxes of Excel's Chart Wizard

- Create column, bar and pie charts
- Format chart text and change chart colours
- Add and edit data labels
- Move and resize charts
- Change the scale of chart axes

New words

At the end of this chapter you should be able to explain the following terms:

- Chart
- Chart area
- Plot area
- Data point
- Data series
- Data label

Charting: the two steps

You follow two main steps to create a chart in Excel:

- Select the cells with contents you want to chart.

- Select and run Excel's Chart Wizard.

Excel chart

A graphic or diagram based on the numbers, text and calulations that are located in the rows and columns of an Excel worksheet.

The four dialog boxes to an Excel chart

When you run the Chart Wizard, Excel presents you with a series of four dialog boxes. These are:

- **Chart Type:** Excel offers lots of different chart types. You decide which is best for your data.

- **Chart Source Data:** What data do you want to chart – all the cells on your worksheet, or just a selected cell range?

- **Chart Options:** How do you want your chart to look? Excel offers a variety of options.

- **Chart Location:** Where do you want the chart stored – on your current worksheet, on a different worksheet, or in a new workbook? You decide.

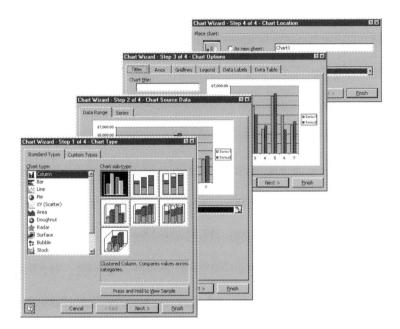

Does this seem like a lot of dialog boxes to learn about? Don't worry. All four dialogs offer a default option that in most cases will create an impressive-looking, ECDL-test-passing chart. So, when in doubt, just click the **Next** button on the first three dialog boxes, and the **Finish** button on the fourth.

Perform Exercise 6.1 to make yourself familiar with charting in Excel.

Exercise 6.1: Creating a simple Excel chart

1 Open the workbook that you saved in Chapter 5 and click on Sheet2 to display its second worksheet.

2 Select the non-adjacent cell range A4:A11, C4:C11.

Do this by clicking in A4, dragging the mouse down to A11, and releasing the mouse button. Next, hold down the Ctrl key, click in cell C4 and drag down to C11.

	A	B	C
4			**January**
5	Conway	John	£2,356.00
6	Higgins	Tracey	£3,463.00
7	Murphy	Robert	£4,921.00
8	Rafferty	Aidan	£2,512.00
9	Smith	Catherine	£5,951.00
10	Smith	Zowie	£3,872.00
11	Sullivan	Andrew	£2,903.00

3 See the button towards the right on the Standard toolbar? That's Excel's Chart Wizard button. Click on it.

4 Excel displays a series of four dialog boxes. On the first three, click the **Next** button. On the fourth and last, click **Finish**.

Excel's Chart Wizard button

Congratulations. You have drawn your first chart in Excel!

Chart area: To move your chart to a different position on your worksheet, click here and drag with the mouse

Plot area: The area of the plotted chart

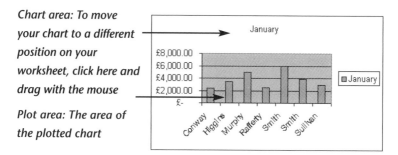

5 Unfortunately, Excel positions your chart on top of your data, so you cannot see both at the same time.

Move the chart by clicking on any blank part of the chart margin – Excel calls this the chart area – and then dragging the chart down until its top-left corner is positioned over the cell B19.

Chart area

The margin area inside the chart boundaries but outside the actual plotted chart. It typically holds labels identifying the chart axes.

To move your chart to a different position on the worksheet, click anywhere on the chart area and drag with the mouse. To delete a chart, click anywhere on the chart area and press the **Delete** key.

Plot area

The area containing the actual plot. It is bounded by the two chart axes and is enclosed withn the chart area.

Charts: two ideas you need to know

All charting – in Excel or with pen and paper – is based on two very basic ideas: the *data point* and the *data series*. You will see these two terms a lot on Excel's charting dialog boxes and online help screens. Understand these two ideas and you will be able to exploit fully Excel's charting possibilities.

About data points

Data point: the idea is so simple that you will wonder why anyone bothered even to give it a name. Consider the four examples below.

Item	Value		Item	Value
Apples	4		January	£ 1,965.34
Pears	3		February	£ 2,451.50
Bananas	6		March	£ 8,301.49

Item	Value		Item	Value
Mary	15.00%		Sales	£4,954,032.00
Catherine	50.00%		Costs	£394,823.00
Margaret	35.00%		Overheads	£25,068.00

Each example consists of individual items (or people) being measured. They are types of fruit, months of the year, people and amounts of money.

Each item has a number that is its measured value. A *data point* is a single item and its numerical value.

In the first example, the three data points are: Apples and 4, Pears and 3 and Bananas and 6. Other data points from the above examples are February and £2,451.50, Catherine and 50%, and Overheads and £25,068.00

A data point always has two parts: the item and the value. On its own, a number is not a data point, nor is an item. You need both for a data point.

Data point

An item being measured and its measured value.

About data series

A single data point does not tell us very much. A chart is useful only if there is more than one data point. A collection of data points is called a data series.

For instance, you may want to create a chart that shows the company's sales figures for different months. Or a chart that compares one month's sales figures for different departments.

Data series

A group of related data points. For example, your data series may compare different items measured at the same time, or a single item measured at different times.

Single data series charts

We used the word 'simple' to describe the chart that you created in Exercise 6.1. More precisely, it is an example of a single data series chart.

Exercise 6.2: Creating more single data series charts

1   Practise your charting skills by selecting the four non-adjacent cell ranges below and creating a chart from them.

2   Drag the first chart down beneath the chart from Exercise 6.1. Then drag the other three down Sheet2 so that each is positioned beneath the previous one.

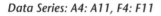

Data Series: A4: A11, F4: F11   *Data Series: A4: A11, I4, I411*

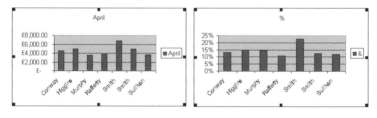

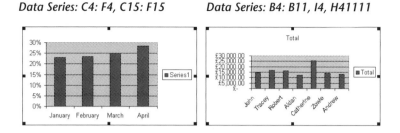

Data Series: C4: F4, C15: F15   *Data Series: B4: B11, I4, H41111*

Creating a multiple data series chart

You can have more than one data series in a collection of related information.

	January	February
Conway	IR£ 2,356.00	IR£ 3,621.00
Higgins	IR£ 3,463.00	IR£ 3,981.00
Murphy	IR£ 4,921.00	IR£ 4,055.00
Rafferty	IR£ 2,512.00	IR£ 2,864.00
Smith	IR£ 3,872.00	IR£ 2,441.00
Smith	IR£ 5,951.00	IR£ 6,226.00
Sullivan	IR£ 2,903.00	IR£ 3,308.00

Consider the part of your worksheet shown on the right. How many data series can you see? Answer: two.

There is one data series for January, and a second for February.

	January			February
Conway	IR£ 2,356.00		Conway	IR£ 3,621.00
Higgins	IR£ 3,463.00		Higgins	IR£ 3,981.00
Murphy	IR£ 4,921.00		Murphy	IR£ 4,055.00
Rafferty	IR£ 2,512.00		Rafferty	IR£ 2,864.00
Smith	IR£ 3,872.00		Smith	IR£ 2,441.00
Smith	IR£ 5,951.00		Smith	IR£ 6,226.00
Sullivan	IR£ 2,903.00		Sullivan	IR£ 3,308.00

Two data series, one for each of the two months

In Exercise 6.3 and 6.4 you will create a two-data series and a three-data series chart.

Exercise 6.3: Creating a two-data series chart in Excel

1   Select the cell range A4:A8, C4:D8.

2   Click the Chart Wizard button and accept the default options in the sequence of four dialog boxes. Your chart should look as shown below.

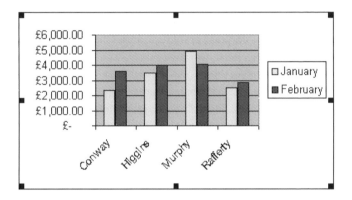

3   Drag your chart down the worksheet to beneath the last of the four charts that you created in Exercise 6.2.

When Excel draws a chart with more than a single data series, it uses a different colour to represent each series.

Exercise 6.4: Creating a three-data series chart in Excel

1   Select the cell range A4:A8, C4:E8.

2   Click on the Chart Wizard button and accept the default options in the sequence of four dialog boxes. Your chart should look as shown opposite.

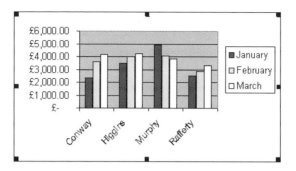

3   Drag the chart down the worksheet to beneath the
    chart that you created in Exercise 6.3.

Editing your chart

When you create a chart, don't think of it as fixed forever.
You can change just about every aspect of a chart.

Changing chart data

You can amend the content of worksheet cells on which your
chart is based; as soon as you change the cells in your
worksheet, Excel updates the chart to reflect your changes.

Resizing the chart

Changing your chart's size can affect its appearance
dramatically. To resize a chart:

*   Click once on the chart area. Handles (small black
    squares) appear around the chart's edges.

*   Click on any handle and hold down the mouse button
    as you drag the chart to a different shape.

If you drag on a corner handle, the chart expands and contracts proportionately to its current size; if you drag on an edge handle, the chart expands or contracts in that direction only. Excel automatically adjusts the font of chart text as you resize.

Changing the chart title

To edit the chart title, click anywhere on it, and then click anywhere within the title text. You can now edit the text. To remove the chart title, click on it once, and press Delete. To reformat the chart title, double-click anywhere on it to display the Format Chart Title dialog box. Select the options you require from the three tabs of the dialog box: Borders and Patterns, Font, and Alignment.

Adding a chart title

If your chart does not have a title, you can add one as follows:

- Right-click on the chart area.

- From the pop-up menu displayed, choose **Chart Options**, select the Titles tab, type the new title in the Chart title: box, and click **OK**.

Chart title

   Text describing the chart. By default, Excel centres the chart title in the chart area over the plot area.

Adding data labels

In an Excel chart, a data label is an item showing the name (such as Conway) or value (such as £2,356.00) of a data point in a plotted data series. By default, Excel does not display labels.

You can add two kinds of data labels to a chart:

- **Value labels**: These indicate the numerical values of the individual data points. See Exercise 6.5.

- **Text labels**: These display the names of the data points. By default, Excel already displays these names on an axis. See Exercise 6.6.

Exercise 6.5: Adding data labels

1 On Sheet2, click on the chart area of the first chart you created, the one in Exercise 4.65, and press Ctrl+c to copy it to the clipboard.

2 Click the Sheet3 tab to display the third worksheet of your workbook. Click cell B3 and press Ctrl+v to paste the chart from the clipboard.

3 Right-click on the chart area, choose **Chart Options** from the pop-up menu, and select the Data Labels tab of the dialog box.

4 Select the Show value option, and click **OK**.

Adding data labels to your chart provides more information to the reader, but has the disadvantage of making your chart more cluttered. You can remedy this by stretching the chart horizontally.

5   Click the chart, and then click the middle handle on the right edge of the chart area.

6   Drag with the mouse until the chart's right boundary ends in column K. The axes and plot area of your chart should look as shown below.

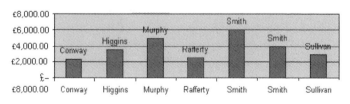

Exercise 6.6: Adding data name labels

1   With the chart from Exercise 6.1 still in the clipboard, click on a cell beneath the chart pasted in Exercise 6.5, and press Ctrl+v. Right-click on the chart area, choose **Chart Options** from the pop-up menu, and select the Data Labels tab of the dialog box.

2   Select the Show label option, and click **OK**.

3   As in Exercise 6.5, drag the chart's right boundary to column K. The axes and plot area of your chart should look as shown below.

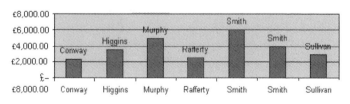

Formatting data labels

To format data labels, right-click on a label, choose **Format |
Data Labels** from the pop-up menu, and select your required
options from the following four dialog box tabs: Patterns,
Font, Number, and Alignment.

Data label

> *The name or numerical value of a data point in a plotted
> data series.*

Changing the scale

To change the scale of an axis, right-click anywhere along the
axis and choose **Format Axis** from the pop-up menu,

Excel allows you to change the minimum, maximum and
increment values displayed for each axis, and the point at
which the two axes cross. In Exercise 6.7 you will change the
scale of a chart's vertical (or Y) axis.

Exercise 6.7: Changing the scale of the vertical axis

1 Is the first chart you created, the one in Exercise 6.1, still
   in the clipboard? If not, copy it to the clipboard now.

2 Click the Sheet3 tab to display the third worksheet of
   your workbook. Click on a cell beneath the chart pasted
   in Exercise 6.6, and press Ctrl+v.

3 Click the chart, and then click on the middle handle on
   its lower edge. Drag down the mouse until the chart is
   about twice its original height.

4 Double-click anywhere on the chart's vertical axis and, on the Format Axis dialog box, select the Scale tab.

5 Change the Minimum: box from 0 to 2000. And change the value in the Major unit: box from its default to 500. Click **OK** to close the dialog box.

6 Double-click again anywhere on the chart's vertical axis, and, on the Format Axis dialog box, reselect the Scale tab.

Notice that Excel has changed the Category (X) axis Crosses at: box from 0 to 2000. This is because you changed the Minimum: box from 0 to 2000.

The rescaled and vertically stretched chart should now look as shown.

Rescaled chart: Vertical axis values begin at £2,000 rather than £0. Also, vertical axis is expressed in units of £500 rather than £2,000.

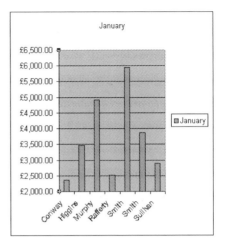

Changing chart colours

Excel enables you to change the colours of three parts of a chart: the chart area, the plot area and the data series. In each case, you right-click on the relevant element, choose the **Format** command from the pop-up menu, and select your required fill colour. See Exercise 6.8.

Exercise 6.8: Changing a chart's colours

1   Right-click on the chart area of the chart you created in Exercise 6.7.

    (The chart area is the blank margin surrounding the actual plotted chart.)

2   Choose the **Format Chart Area** command from the pop-up menu, select the Patterns tab, click the colour Yellow in the Area section of the dialog box, and click **OK**.

3   Right-click on the plot area of the chart.
(This is the actual plotted chart, bounded by the two chart axes.)

4   Choose the **Format Plot Area** command from the pop-up menu, click the colour Yellow in the Area section of the dialog box, and click **OK**.

5   Right-click on any of the chart columns.
(The columns represent the data series of the chart.)

6   Choose the **Format Data Series** command from the pop-up menu, select the Patterns tab, click the colour Red in the Area section of the dialog box, and click **OK**.

In the second part of this exercise, you will reformat the text elements of the chart.

7   Double-click the X-(horizontal) axis, select the Font tab, change the font to Bold and the Font Colour to dark blue, and click **OK**.

8   Repeat step 7 for the Y-(vertical) axis, but do not close the dialog box.

9   With the Y-axis still selected, select the Number tab on the Format Axis dialog box, and set the number of decimal places to zero. Click **OK**.

10 Right-click on the chart title, choose the **Format Chart Title** command from the pop-up menu, select the Font tab, change the Font to Times New Roman, Font Style to Italic and Font Size to 14 point.

11 With the chart title still selected, select the Patterns tab of the dialog box, select the Automatic Border option, and click **OK**.

Well done. You have completed the exercise. Your chart should now look as shown.

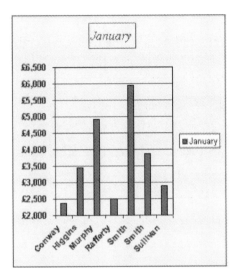

Chart types

Excel offers over a dozen chart types, but you need only know the following three:

- **Column chart**: Items are shown horizontally and values vertically. This is Excel's default chart type, and the only one you have used in your charting exercises so far.

- **Bar chart**: A 'sideways' column chart that shows items vertically and values horizontally.

- **Pie chart**: Shows the proportion that each item contributes to the total. Unlike column, bar and most other chart types, you can use pie charts for a single data series only.

Setting the chart type

When you select a cell range and choose the Chart Wizard, you decide which chart type you want to use in the first of the four dialog boxes displayed by the Wizard, the Chart Type box. As you can see, most chart types offer sub-types or variations.

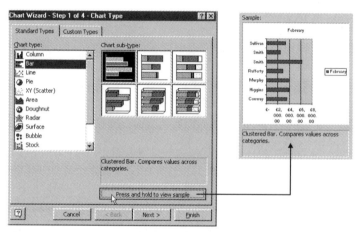

You can preview how your data will look in a particular chart type by selecting a Chart type option and clicking the Press and hold to view sample button

Changing chart type

To change the current type of a chart, right-click anywhere within the chart (chart area, plot area or data series – it does not matter), choose the **Chart Type** command from the pop-up menu, and select a different type (or sub-type) from the Chart Type dialog box.

In Exercise 6.9 you will create a new chart of the bar chart type. In Exercise 6.10 you will change a bar chart to a column one.

Exercise 6.9: Creating a bar chart

1 On Sheet3, click on a cell beneath the chart you worked with in Exercise 6.8. This will be the location at which the chart you create in this exercise will begin.

2 Click the Sheet1 tab to display the first worksheet of your workbook.

3 Select non-adjacent cell range C25:D26, F25:G26, and click the Chart Wizard button.

4 Excel now displays the Standard Types tab of the Chart Wizard – Step 1 of 4 – Chart Type dialog box. Select the Bar Chart type and click **Next**.

5 Excel now displays the Data Range tab of the Chart Wizard – Step 2 of 4 – Chart Source Data dialog box. Click **Next**.

6 Excel now displays the Chart Wizard – Step 3 of 4 – Chart Options dialog box.

Click the Titles tab, and type a Chart title of Product 1 and click **Next**.

Chart Wizard - Step 3 of 4 - Chart Options   `?` `X`

| Titles | Axes | Gridlines | Legend | Data Labels | Data Table |

Chart title:

Product 1

Category (X) axis:

Value (Y) axis:

Second category (X) axis:

Second value (Y) axis:

Product 1

Price
Discount
Variable
Fixed

0   5   10   15   20   25

■ Series 1

`?`   Cancel   < Back   Next >   Finish

7   Excel now displays the Chart Wizard – Step 4 of 4 –
Chart Location dialog box.

Change the As object in: box to Sheet3 and click **Finish**.

Chart Wizard - Step 4 of 4 - Chart Location   `?` `X`

Place chart:

⚬ As new sheet: Chart1

⦿ As object in: Sheet3

`?`   Cancel   < Back   Next >   Finish

Excel positions the chart on your third worksheet,
Sheet3. It positions the chart so that its top-left corner is
at the cell you most recently clicked on in that
worksheet. Your bar chart should look like that shown.

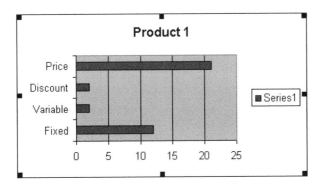

Exercise 6.10: Changing a column to a bar chart

1   On Sheet2, click the third chart you created in Exercise 6.2. It is based on the cell range C4:F4,C15:F15. Copy it to the clipboard.

2   Click the Sheet3 tab to display your third worksheet. Paste the chart from the clipboard to a cell beneath the chart from Exercise 6.9.

3   Right-click on the chart area, choose Chart Type from the pop-up menu, select Bar chart from the dialog box, and click **OK**   .

Your bar chart should look like that shown.

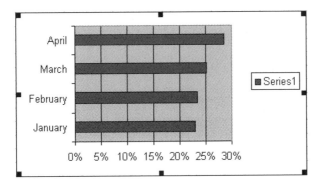

Working with pie charts

In Exercise 6.11 you will create a pie chart based on a single data series. You will then format the pie chart, and 'explode' a slice of the pie to draw particular attention to the contribution it represents to the total.

Exercise 6.11: Creating and formatting a pie chart

1   On Sheet2, select the cell range A4:A11, C4:C11.

2   Click the Chart Wizard button.

3   In the Chart Type dialog box, select Pie chart as the Chart type, and Pie with a 3D visual effect as the sub-type. Click **Next**.

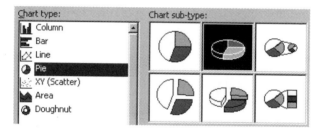

4   On the remaining Chart Wizard dialog boxes, click **Next** and, finally, **Finish**.

Drag the pie chart down Sheet2 to beneath the chart you created in Exercise 6.4. Your chart should look as shown.

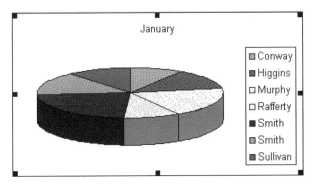

Because pie charts do not have axes to indicate data point names and values, the various slices are typically accompanied by data labels. You will add these in the next steps of this exercise.

5 Double-click on the pie chart plot area (and not the surrounding chart area) to display the Format Data Series dialog box.

6 Select the Data Labels tab, select the option Show percent, and click **OK**. Your pie chart should now look as below. Notice how the plot area shrank in size to make room for the percentage data labels.

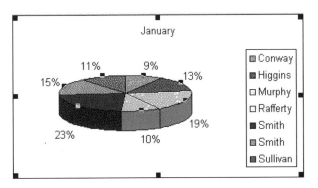

In the final step of this exercise, you will 'explode' one slice of the pie chart.

7 Click once in the plot area of the pie chart. Next, click on
the slice you want to explode and drag it out of the pie.

For example, click the largest slice, the one with 23%
data label, and drag it down and to the left.

Your pie chart should now look as shown.

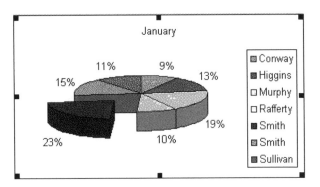

Congratulations. You have now completed Chapter 6 on
charting with Excel. You may close and save your workbook,
and close Excel.

Chapter summary: so now you know

To draw a chart in Excel, first select the cells with the
numbers and text that you want to chart, and then run
Excel's *Chart Wizard*. The Wizard's default options in its four
dialog boxes are acceptable in most cases. If you change
any of the data on which a chart is based, Excel updates the
chart to reflect the changes.

By default, Excel positions your chart on top of your
worksheet data. You can move the chart by clicking on any
blank part of the chart margin, and then dragging the chart
to a new position.

Charting is based on the ideas of data points and data series. A *data point* is a single item and its related value (for example, the sales figure in January), while a *data series* is a group of related data points (for example, monthly sales figures over a year). You can chart more than one data series at a time.

Excel offers a wide range of *chart types*, with column, bar and pie charts being the most commonly used. You can *format* your chart in a variety of ways by adding data labels, colours and borders.

CHAPTER 7

File formats and data importing

In this chapter

In this chapter you will learn how Excel 2000 uses a particular file format. You will also discover how to convert your documents into other, non-Excel 2000 file formats, so that they can be opened and read by people who work with applications other than Excel 2000.

You will also discover how files containing images, graphs and text may be inserted into Excel worksheets.

New skills

At the end of this chapter you should be able to:

- Save Excel 2000 files in the following file formats: Excel 2000 templates, earlier versions of Excel, non-Excel spreadsheets, databases, text-only and HTML (Web format)
- Explain the difference between character-delimited and column-delimited text files

- Explain the difference between two types of character-delimited text files: tab-delimited and comma-separated
- Insert image files in an Excel worksheet, and files containing graphs created in applications other than Excel 2000
- Import text files using Excel's Text Import Wizard

New words

At the end of this chapter you should be able to explain the following terms:
- File format
- Tab-delimited text file
- Comma-separated values (CSV) text file
- Column-delimited text file

File formats

In ECDL Module 1 you learnt how all information stored on a computer consists ultimately of just two characters: 1 and 0. This raises two, related, questions:

- When you open an Excel workbook file, how are these 1s and 0s translated into the text, numbers and charts you see on your computer screen?

- And, when you save a file, how are the text, numbers and charts converted back to 1s and 0s on your computer?

The answer is that the application developers apply a set of rules that translate between the 1s and 0s and the displayed text, numbers and charts. Such a set of rules is called a file format.

File format

> *A set of rules that translates 1s and 0s into text and graphics on computers screens and printouts, and vice versa.*

An Excel file, for example, is said to be in Excel file format; an Access file in Access file format, and so on.

Different applications, different file formats

Different software companies, however, use different sets of rules for translating 1s and 0s into the text and graphics on screens and printouts.

Moreover, different versions of the one application often use different file formats. The Microsoft Excel 2000 file format, for example, is different from the file formats of some earlier versions of Excel.

These different file formats, as you can imagine, can create problems:

- In one file format, for example, the characters 10101010 might translate as the number '12' positioned in cell A4.

- In another, the same characters of 10101010 might convert to the label 'Annual Profit' in cell Z54.

File name extensions

The format of a file is revealed by its three-letter file name extension, which the software application adds to the file name when the user saves the file.

The file name extension of .xls, for example, indicates an Excel workbook, and .mdb an Access database.

The file format used in pages on the world wide web is HTML, which stands for HyperText Markup Language. HTML file names typically end in .htm or .html.

Excel's file format options

Excel 2000 offers you the ability to save your documents in a format other than its own. This feature is very useful when you want to provide a file you have created to someone who uses an application other than Excel 2000.

To view the file formats in which you can save your Excel 2000 documents:

- Open a document.

- Choose **File | Save As**.

- Click on the arrow to the right of the Save as type: box.

File name:	Book1.xls	▼
Save as type:	Microsoft Excel Workbook (*.xls)	▼
	Microsoft Excel Workbook (*.xls)	▲
	Template (*.xlt)	
	Formatted Text (Space delimited) (*.prn)	
	Text (Tab delimited) (*.txt)	
	Microsoft Excel 5.0/95 Workbook (*.xls)	
	Microsoft Excel 97 & 5.0/95 Workbook (*.xls)	▼

Only some of the listed options are relevant to this ECDL Spreadsheet module. Note that the features and formatting of a Microsoft Excel 2000 workbook might not be available if you save the workbook in the file format of a previous version of Microsoft Excel or of another application.

Excel template

Excel 2000 offers you the ability to save a workbook as a template. You can then use the saved template as a basis for quickly creating other, similar workbooks.

For example, you could create a workbook for use as an expense form, enter and format relevant text labels, place borders around certain cells, and enter the function =SUM(C2:C22) in cell C23 so that whatever numbers were typed in the range C2:C22 are totalled and displayed in C23.

By saving such a workbook as a template, you speed up the process of creating further expense forms because the text, formatting and addition calculation need not be re-entered.

To save a workbook as a template, choose **File | Save As** and select the Template (*.xlt) option.

Previous Excel versions

You can save your Excel 2000 workbook in the file formats of previous versions of Microsoft Excel. You have two main options:

- A format that can be read by Excel 5.0 and Excel 95

- A format that can be read by Excel 5.0, Excel 95 and Excel 97

dBASE, Lotus 1-2-3 and Quattro Pro formats

Select from these options to save your work so that it can be opened and read by users with versions of Lotus 1-2-3 or Quattro Pro (two other spreadsheet applications) or dBASE (a database application).

Only the currently displayed worksheet is converted. To convert other worksheets of a workbook, display and then save each one individually.

Text-only format

As its name suggests, this format saves only the text of a file. The word 'text' in this context includes numbers as well as alphabetic characters. All formatting is lost. This format is also called plain-text or ASCII format.

Two of the more commonly used plain-text options
are as follows:

- **Text (tab-delimited):** This saves only the currently
  displayed worksheet. To convert other worksheets of a
  workbook, switch to each sheet and save it separately.
  The file name extension added is .txt.

  In this format, cell entries in the same row but in different
  columns are separated from each other by tabs. Different
  rows are separated by paragraph breaks. As you can see in
  the example below, text in the tab-delimited format does
  not necessarily line up vertically in neat columns.

Original data in Excel file

*Excel worksheet saved in tab-delimited format, and viewed in Notepad
text editor*

- **CSV (comma-delimited):** Similar to tab-delimited, but
  with a comma rather than a tab separating cells on the
  same row. The file name extension added is .csv,
  meaning comma-separated values.

Excel worksheet in CSV format, and viewed in Notepad text editor

Tab-delimited text file

A text-format file in which data items are separated horizontally by tabs and vertically by paragraph breaks.

Comma-separated values (CSV) text file

A text-format file in which data items are separated horizontally by commas and vertically by paragraph breaks.

HTML (web) format

Web pages are created using the HTML file format. The file name extension of this format is .htm (or, sometimes, .html).

You can save an Excel 2000 file in HTML format in either of two ways:

- Choose **File | Save As Web page**.

–or–

- Choose **File | Save As**, and select the web Page option.

The worksheet cells are converted to table cells in the HTML file. You can display and print HTML format files with a web browser application such as Microsoft Internet Explorer or Netscape Navigator.

Inserting from other applications

Microsoft Office applications (and most other Windows applications) allow you to transfer information between them. For this ECDL Spreadsheet module, you need know only how to insert images, graphics and text in Excel.

Inserting images

To insert an image, choose **Insert | Picture**, and then select the relevant option. The range of options available to you depends on whether you have installed the Microsoft Office Clip Art Gallery and whether a scanner is attached to your computer.

- To *reposition* an inserted image, click on it to select it, and then drag the image to a different part of your worksheet.

- To *resize* an inserted image, click on it to select it, then click any sizing handle and drag the image to a different shape.

If you drag on a corner handle, the image expands and contracts proportionately to its current size; if you drag on an edge handle, the image expands or contracts in that direction only. Other inserted objects can be repositioned and resized in the same way.

Exercise 7.1: Inserting an image file in Excel

To insert an image in a worksheet, you need an image to work with. If you do not have one to hand, follow steps 1 and 2 of this exercise to obtain one from the author's website.

1   Connect to the internet, start Microsoft Internet Explorer or Netscape Navigator, and visit the author's website at <u>www.munnelly.com</u>.

2   Right-click on the image at the top-left of the first page to display a pop-up menu, choose **Save Picture As** (or, in Netscape, **Save Image As**), and save the image file to your computer as munnelly_com.jpg.

3   Display an Excel worksheet, click on a cell, choose **Insert | Picture| From File**, locate the munnelly_com.jpg image file (or any other image file), and click **Insert**.

Excel inserts the image as shown below.

Inserting graphs

Graphs can be created in applications other than Excel – for example, in Microsoft PowerPoint or in non-Microsoft applications. To insert such a graph, select it in the application in which it was created, copy it to the clipboard, open the Excel worksheet and choose the **Edit | Paste** command.

Inserting text

You may want to insert two types of text into an Excel worksheet:

- **Small amounts of text**: You may want to select one or a few words from a text file for use in Excel as worksheet headings, for example, or as labels for individual cells.

  To insert text in a single cell of a worksheet, open the application in which the text was created, copy the text to the clipboard, switch to Excel, and then use Excel's **Edit | Paste** command to insert it in a selected Excel cell.

- **An entire text file**: This may contain numbers as well as text characters, which you will want Excel to 'interpret' and arrange correctly across rows and down columns.

To assist you inserting a text file in this way, Excel provides a Text Import Wizard.

Text Import Wizard

Earlier in this chapter you learnt about tab-delimited and comma-separated text files in which the tab and comma characters are positioned within the file to indicate where one column of data ends and the next begins. These are called *character-delimited* files, because a specific character (either tab or comma) consistently indicates column endings.

In other text files, a column ending may be indicated not by a single occurrence of a specific character but by a series of blank spaces. These are called *column-delimited* files, because the blank spaces cause the data to line up vertically. In both types of text files, row endings are indicated by paragraph breaks.

In Exercise 7.2 you will create a tab-delimited file, and in Exercise 7.3 you will import that file using Excel's Text Import Wizard.

Column-delimited text file

A text format file in which data items are separated horizontally by a series of spaces and vertically by paragraph breaks. The blank spaces cause the data to line up vertically.

Exercise 7.2: Creating a Tab-Delimited Text File

1 Using Notepad or other text editor, create a new file.

2 Type the following five words, pressing the Tab key after each word except the last (do not type spaces between the words):

Jan Feb Mar Apr May

3 Press Enter to move the cursor to a new line.

4 Type the following five numbers, pressing the Tab key after each one except the last (do not type spaces between the numbers):

12 45 35 41 56

5 Press Enter to move the cursor to a new line.

6 Type the following five numbers, pressing the Tab key after each one except the last (again, do not type spaces between the numbers):

11 42 34 39 47

```
▤ Book1.txt - Notepad                        _ □ ✕
 File  Edit  Search  Help
January February             March  April   May
12       45       35         41     56
11       42       34         39     47
```

Your file should look as shown. (The columns may not always line up vertically.)

7   Save, name and close your text file.

Exercise 7.3: Importing a tab-delimited text file

1   In Excel, choose **File | Open**, and select the text file saved in Exercise 7.2.

2   Excel displays the first of three Text Import Wizard dialog boxes. Ensure that the field values in the top part of the dialog box are as shown.

Click **Next**.

3   Excel displays the second Text Import Wizard dialog box. Ensure that the field values in the top part of the dialog box are as shown.

Click **Next**.

4 Excel displays the third Text Import Wizard dialog box.
   Ensure that the field values look as shown.

Click **Finish**.

5 Excel closes the Text Import Wizard and displays a
   worksheet that should look similar to that shown. The
   workbook file name will be the same as that of the text file.

6 You can save and close your workbook, and close Excel.

You have now completed the final chapter of the ECDL
Spreadsheets module. Congratulations.

Chapter summary: so now you know

A *file format* is a set of rules that translates between the 1s and 0s used by the computer to store information and the text and graphics displayed on screens and on printouts. Different applications – even different versions of the same application – can use different and incompatible file formats.

To help you share your files with others, Excel 2000 allows you to save your workbooks in a file format other than its own. The options include: earlier versions of Microsoft Excel, Lotus 1-2-3 and Quattro Pro (other spreadsheets), dBASE (a database) and HTML (the web page file format).

Another option is to save an Excel 2000 workbook as an Excel *template*, and re-use any text, numbers, formatting and calculations in the template as a basis for creating further workbooks.

Excel workbooks can also be saved as *text-only* files, with tabs or commas inserted to separate different columns, and paragraph breaks to separate rows.

You can insert image files into an Excel worksheet, and graphs created in other applications. Excel's *Text Import Wizard* assists you in opening text files because it can recognize characters that have been inserted in the text files to separate different columns and rows.